GREEK VEGETARIAN COOKING

Other titles in this series

Indian Vegetarian Cooking
Italian Vegetarian Cooking
Mexican Vegetarian Cooking
Oriental Vegetarian Cooking
Vegetables the French Way

GREEK

VEGETARIAN COOKING

ALKMINI CHAITOW

Illustrated by Clive Birch

HEALING ARTS PRESS

Rochester, Vermont

Healing Arts Press
One Park Street
Rochester, Vermont 05767

Library of Congress Cataloging-in-Publication Data

Chaitow, Alkmini
  Greek vegetarian cooking / by Alkmini Chaitow ; illustrated by
Clive Birch.
    p. cm.
  ISBN 0-89281-340-7 :
  1. Vegetarian Cookery. 2. Cookery, Greek. I. Birch, Clive.
II. Title.
TX837.C437 1989
641.5'636--dc20   89-15547
                                                                CIP

Printed and bound in the United States

10 9 8 7 6 5 4 3 2 1

Healing Arts Press is a division of Inner Traditions International, Ltd.

Distributed to the book trade in the United States by Harper and Row Publishers, Inc.

Distributed to the book trade in Canada by Book Center, Inc., Montreal, Quebec

Distributed to the health food trade in Canada by Alive Books, Toronto and Vancouver

Contents

I dedicate this book to my husband Leon
and our daughter Sasha,
with love.

Acknowledgements

I would like to thank Simon Martin, Editor of *Here's Health* for "pulling the trigger" and encouraging my writing.

I thank my mother, Antigoni Metallinou, for her influence in my cooking.

Finally, I thank my husband Leon for his constant help and support.

Introduction

Some people eat to live; in the West, most people seem to live to eat. Whichever group you fall into, the food described in this book will be found to be ideal. For those who see food as a simple matter of providing the body with its raw materials for the day, these balanced recipes of health-promoting wholefoods will provide many interesting variations. For those to whom the preparing, serving and eating of exciting foods is an important part of their lives, the unique "Greekness" of these recipes will open new vistas. For myself, I can say that the eating of such dishes as *Skordalia* and *Stuffed Squash Blossoms*, to name but two of the recipes included here, have been experiences I will always remember and cherish.

For a variety of reasons more and more people are following a vegetarian pattern of eating, and there is an even greater swing away from over-refined convenience and "junk" foods and towards foods which have undergone a minimum of processing. Such foods have become known as wholefoods, and the advantages of a balanced wholefood and vegetarian diet are now so evident that many nutritionists have ceased to label those that eat this way as cranks or faddists, and instead openly recommend this eating pattern. From a health maintenance point of view, a diet such as this, with its abundance of complex carbohydrates, vegetable proteins, minerals, vitamins, enzymes, fiber and minimum of refined carbohydrates and saturated fats, is demonstrably superior to a "normal" Western diet.

From an ecological standpoint, the vegetarian way of eating, with the emphasis on whole grains, legumes, vegetables and fruits, is one which imposes far less strain on the earth's resources in terms of land and energy requirements for food production. Also, from an aesthetic or humanitarian viewpoint, such a diet is the logical result of compassion for animals and a desire to minimize or end the suffering endured by billions of animals for the sake of a flesh-consuming society.

Since eating and its associated social aspects are an integral part of life, it is important to ensure that a change to a different dietary pattern does not create more problems than it solves. The new diet should provide nutritious and delicious food which, ideally, is not too difficult to prepare or too expensive. Most of the food in this book qualifies in these respects.

I have been a vegetarian for some twenty-five years and have seen my health improve from a reasonable average to a much higher level, despite the slide into middle age. Much of the credit for this must go to the delicious and often inspired culinary gifts of my wife, Alkmini. Born and bred on the magical island of Corfu, she has utilized her knowledge of Mediterranean cooking to add variety and interest to the basic ingredients of vegetarian whole-food cooking. Some of her recipes have been taken from the traditional meatless meals eaten during the Greek Orthodox Lenten period. Others have been adapted from commonly eaten dishes by substituting wholefood vegetarian ingredients for their fish or meat contents. Still others are purely her own invention based on her knowledge of the characteristics of the various ingredients used in a wholefood diet.

Having had no formal culinary training, her instinctive awareness of which foods blend together, both in taste and texture, has been enhanced by her knowledge of the nutritional value of the foods available to a vegetarian. Knowing of the many individuals who are unable to eat dairy products, Alkmini has successfully experimented with alternatives such as soy milk. As a result, such dishes as Millet Pie, for example, can be enjoyed by anyone with a milk allergy by using soy milk to make the delicious Béchamel Sauce (see page 42).

The recipes in this book will open new horizons for many vegetarians whose meals may have become less than exciting. For those who are feeling their way towards this vegetarianism, the recipes will provide meals, the enjoyment of which will soon blot out past habits in a deluge of new flavors and textures.

The basic pattern of eating that I have found most conducive to the promotion and maintenance of health is one in which one of the two main meals, midday or evening, is a raw salad-type meal and the other a cooked protein savory-type meal. With the salad meal it is essential, I believe, to maintain interest by including a variety of textures and tastes. The salad recipes will enhance these aspects of anyone's raw food intake. The protein (cooked) meal, which should be accompanied by cooked or raw vegetables, can contain animal protein in the form of eggs, cheese or milk, or consist completely of vegetable foods. If no animal protein is present in the ingredients of such a meal (and, personally, this is the ideal I would aim for) then in order that the body gets its necessary protein there must be a combination of legumes and cereals. Legumes such as lentils, chickpeas and lima beans, and cereals such as millet, wholegrain wheat, brown rice, etc., will provide all the required protein and amino acids when eaten at the same meal.

My own breakfast recommendation is a wholegrain cereal, seeds (sunflower, pumpkin etc.) and fruit (fresh and dried) mixture with natural yogurt.

In this book Alkmini has not only provided recipes, but also some menu suggestions and patterns of eating which should help guide the newcomer towards a balanced intake of these lovely foods. Food should be fun, and what a bonus if it is also good for you! The Mediterranean people enjoy their food, and mealtimes are pleasant family or social gatherings. By adding the extra dimension of wholeness to the food and by adapting many of the region's delicacies to meet the needs of vegetarians, I believe many people will enjoy new and exciting mealtime experiences, while also building and maintaining healthier bodies.

Western civilization owes much to Greece in terms of its heritage, whether it be language, ideas or morals. With this contribution to the culinary arts, the debt to her is just a little bit greater.

LEON CHAITOW
N.D., D.O., M.B.N.O.A.

1. General Instructions

Cooking should not be drudgery. Perhaps it is repetitive, in that day follows day and meal follows meal, seemingly without end. When thinking about cooking, therefore, it helps to consider the creative aspect of the art, as well as the pleasure and nourishment which the effort will bring to family or friends. The environment in which the food is prepared and cooked should be pleasant. This will be helped by organizing a clean and tidy kitchen. Such details as a colorful apron, a small vase with one or two flowers, a little background music, and so on, all help to make the humblest kitchen into a pleasant little kingdom in which to create the alchemy of good cooking.

After selecting the recipe, the next step is to gather together all the ingredients on the working surface. Individual plates and containers should hold the various prescribed quantities. This may seem obvious, but it is surprising how many recipes go wrong because halfway through the preparation, something essential is found to be missing. It pays to be methodical and to work slowly. For example, washing each dish and saucepan as it is used saves a great deal of effort later.

Once the food is prepared and cooking, it should not be left for more than a minute or two. This time can be spent tidying up and cleaning, all the while keeping an eye on the food. The result will be a tidier kitchen, and the cooking food will not be in danger of burning.

Results may, from time to time, be disappointing. This is unlikely to be the fault of the recipe, but more probably a result of too much water having been used, or the wrong amount of seasoning (too much or too little), or the heat used may have been too high or too low. The best advice is to use your common sense and try again, adapting and experimenting by all means, but only when the basic recipe has been successfully mastered.

It is certainly a good idea, when guests are expected, to use only recipes that you have previously mastered. This helps to avoid tension, aggravation, disappointment, and embarrassment.

Cooking Vegetables the Greek Way

The advantage of cooking vegetables the Greek way (boiling until soft) is that they can be served cold. This means that preparation can take place some hours prior to serving them. The flavor of cooked vegetables, served cold, is superior to that of hot vegetables, but they will have lost something of their nutritive value. Cooking vegetables for cold serving is simply a matter of bring a saucepan of salted water to the boil, adding the vegetables and cooking until tender. These should be drained, placed on a serving dish, and dressed with olive oil and lemon juice before serving, cold, when required. Garnish with black olives for additional flavor.

Steaming Vegetables (Not the Greek Way)

When hot cooked vegetables are needed for a meal, they should be prepared just prior to serving. In Greece, the majority of people boil vegetables until they are very soft. This method might be traditional, but is not ideal for retaining nutritional value or for producing really tasty vegetables. If the aim is to achieve tasty dishes, full of nutritional goodness, which retain their freshness, crispness and color, then the ideal cooking method is steaming.

Place the vegetables in a steamer. Depending upon the type of vegetable, more or less time will be required. Cauliflower and zucchini, for example, require five to seven minutes, whereas globe artichokes, carrots, Brussels sprouts, etc., need a few minutes more. For a delicious flavor-enhancer, add a dressing of olive oil and lemon juice (two parts oil to one part lemon, and a little salt) to the cooked vegetables just before serving.

The *Skordalia* dish (page 18) complements any cooked vegetable. If *Skordalia* is not available, then one or two cloves of raw garlic sliced thinly on the vegetables makes for a fantastic, flavorsome experience; this is real "peasant" style food. As for the odor, friends might not appreciate the garlic, but your heart certainly will. It is worth noting that *the lowest incidence of heart disease in the world occurs in Corfu*. The use of olive oil and garlic in large amounts is thought to be the main reason for this.

A Few Tips

- When preparing globe artichokes, the fingers tend to discolor to a dirty brown shade. Rubbing your hands with half a lemon will remove this.

- After eating garlic brush your teeth and chew some parsley. This should help to remove, or at least to reduce, the odor.

- To give a brown color to vegetable soup or broth, add to the cooking contents in the saucepan some outer leaves of onion. These should be removed before serving.

- Lemon juice can be available all year round by freezing it, as ice cubes, and storing in plastic bags in the freezer.

- Bread keeps fresh when kept in the refrigerator.

- When lemons are very fresh or not terribly juicy, they may be hard. It is much easier to squeeze the juice out of them if they are first rolled and pressed on a hard surface before cutting.

- In Greece, we use a bowl of cow's milk to remove undesirable smells from the refrigerator. Place the bowl with the milk in it and leave for a day or so, before discarding.

- In order to minimize the sharpness of some varieties of onions, the onion slices should be placed in a bowl containing water and a little cider vinegar. These should soak for half an hour to an hour. The taste of the onion should then be sweeter.

- To avoid 'crying' when peeling onions, leave the root untouched until the rest of the onion has been sliced. Amazing as it seems, this simple measure does prevent this common kitchen discomfort.

- When wishing to thaw something from the freezer, do so by transferring it to the refrigerator. Thawing in a hurry spoils the flavor and might result in the idea that the particular food does not freeze well.

- Potatoes are widely used in Greek cooking. Apart from the obvious ways, there are several specialities such as Potato Salad and Skordalia (mashed potatoes with garlic and lemon), which are uniquely Greek. When the intention is to make either Potato Salad or Skordalia, it is recommended that they first be boiled in salted water. The quality of the potatoes can, of course, affect the quality of the resulting dish.
  If you wish to find out which potatoes are particularly starchy (and therefore better for the purpose of mashing or mixing, as in Skordalia), then cut a potato in half and rub the two halves together. If, in doing so, a lot of juice is evident then this indicates that the potatoes contain a lot of water and would probably split in cooking. If, on the other hand, a frothy, thick, liquid is produced by rubbing the two halves together, this indicates a higher starch content, and therefore a "better" potato. (This useful little trick was shown to me by my very old-fashioned grandmother some twenty-five years ago).

- Never use any potatoes that are green. These are dangerous in any quantity and can cause upsets, even in small amounts. Avoid using sprouting potatoes and never use any potato tops or their flowers.

2. Mezze Dishes (Appetizers)

Mezze in the Greek language means "bits and pieces" of appetizing foods. By the time a guest has finished the "appetizers", so much has usually been eaten that the appetite is fully satisfied. This type of "meal" would be ideal for a party or as a variation from the normal – perhaps eaten outdoors on a summer evening.

On individual little plates serve the following:

Tjatjiki (page 18)
Roasted Lima Beans (page 95)
Stuffed Squash Blossoms (page 79)
Potato Salad (page 103)
Beet Salad (page 104)
Hummus (page 23)
Eggplant Dip (page 22)
Chickpea Croquettes (page 101)
Cheeses
Black olives
Radishes and radish tops
Scallions
Lettuce leaves
Cucumber sticks
Wholewheat bread

GARLIC POTATO
Skordalia

(Enough for several meals) *Gluten and Dairy-free*
This is a tasty relish or side dish. The virtues of garlic are
well known – it is credited with anti-catarrhal qualities, it
is said to lower the blood-pressure, to be anti-rheumatic
and to lower cholesterol levels; it is often cited as a "blood
purifier". These valuable assets added to the nutritive
value of lemon juice (vitamin C) and olive oil make this
dish a real health food. Keep surplus refrigerated.

3½ pounds potatoes
2 large heads of garlic, about 1½ ounces each in weight,
    peeled and crushed
Sea salt to taste
4 lemons
1½ cups olive oil
A little parsley
6 black olives
2-3 slices of lemon

Boil the unpeeled potatoes in salted water. Crush the
garlic into an empty mixing bowl. Peel the potatoes and
add them to the bowl *while still hot*. Add a pinch of salt. A
mixer should be used to reduce the potato and garlic
mixture to a pulp. Alternately, add the lemon juice and
olive oil bit by bit until all the ingredients are totally
blended into a smooth mixture. This procedure can be
(and was in the past) carried out by mixing the ingredients
in a mortar and pestle. Such a method has the same result
but is, of course, very hard work.

Place the creamy mixture into a bowl and garnish with
parsley, olives and slices of lemon. This has a very strong
garlic flavor and more or less garlic can be used, according
to taste.

Note:
(a) Skordalia may be served cold as a side dish. It goes
    very well with any vegetable, especially beets.

(b) If the mixture is not creamy (since the quality of potatoes vary) add one to two tablespoons warm water and a little more lemon juice to the mixture.

GARLIC WITH BREAD AND NUTS
Skordalia me Karydia

Dairy-free
This wholesome dip has the nutritive value of nuts with their high mineral content as well as the health-giving qualities of garlic and olive oil. It is ideally used as a dip with salad sticks (carrot, cucumber, celery, radishes).

1 head of garlic, peeled and crushed
2 cups wholewheat bread, soaked and well squeezed
Sea salt
2½ cups olive oil
1 cup walnuts or almonds, well grated
⅓ cup wine vinegar

Place the crushed garlic in the mixing bowl with the bread. Add a little salt and mix well. Then add alternately, a little at a time, the soaked bread, the oil, nuts and vinegar. If you find that the mixture is too thick, add a little warm water. This is a side dish and is served cold.

Note: The texture will, to a large extent, depend on whether an electric mixer or mortar and pestle is used. In both cases, the nuts must be ground first.

YOGURT AND CUCUMBER DIP
Tjatjiki

Gluten-free
This delicious and refreshing summer dip has the nutritive value of yogurt (vitamin B, etc.) as well as the health-giving qualities of garlic and cucumber. Wholewheat bread, cucumber and celery are ideal for dipping into Tjatjiki.

2 cloves crushed garlic (or more to taste)
Sea salt and freshly ground black pepper
2 teaspoonsful olive oil
1 teaspoonful wine vinegar
8 ounces goat's or sheep's milk yogurt
½ a cucumber, coarsely grated

Mix the crushed garlic with the salt and pepper. Add the oil and vinegar and mix well. Place the yogurt in a serving bowl. Add the oil and vinegar mixture in stages, stirring gently with a wooden spoon. Then add the grated cucumber and mix well. Chill before serving.

Note: If the yogurt is very fresh and therefore runny, I suggest that you place the grated cucumber on absorbent paper towels in order to get rid of excess juice before adding it to the yogurt.

TAHINI DIP

Gluten and Dairy-free
This uniquely flavorsome dip has great nutritive value, not only through the proven health-giving properties of olive oil, garlic, parsley and lemon juice, but also in the calcium, iron and thiamin content of sesame seed paste (tahini).

5-6 tablespoons lemon juice
2 cloves of garlic, crushed
3 tablespoons very finely chopped parsley
4 heaped tablespoons tahini (sesame paste from health food stores)
Sea salt

Place all the ingredients together and mix well to a smooth, creamy texture. Serve with toast or fresh whole-wheat bread, celery, and tomatoes.

Note: If the above mixture does not produce a smooth, creamy texture, add a little water.

EGGPLANT DIP
Melitzanosalata

Gluten-free
This tasty dip is ideally served with salad vegetables cut into strips, such as carrots, celery, and cucumber, or with wholewheat bread. The goat's or sheep's cheese and goat's milk make this a protein-rich dish.

2 large eggplants
1½ cups pure olive oil
1 cup goat's milk
Lemon juice to taste
½ cup féta cheese
Sea salt and freshly ground black pepper

Wash, dry and place the eggplants in the oven at 350°F for 1-1½ hours. When cooked, remove and discard the skins. Place the flesh in a mixing bowl and reduce to a creamy texture. This mixture should be worked with a pestle in a mortar, adding alternately the oil, milk and a little lemon. When the mixture is frothy, add the cheese which should already have been crumbled by hand. Season with salt and pepper. Place the mixture in a glass bowl and decorate with small slices of tomato, parsley and black olives.

HUMMUS DIP

Gluten and Dairy-free

Chickpeas (garbanzo beans) have a high protein content (13 per cent) and are rich in potassium, magnesium and iron.

½ cup chickpeas
2 tablespoons tahini (sesame paste from health food stores)
4 tablespoons olive oil
2 cloves of garlic
Sea salt
Lemon juice and lemon slices
Black olives

Soak the chickpeas overnight. Empty the water, add fresh water and then cook before changing the water again. (This eliminates enzymes which can produce flatulence). Allow the chickpeas to cook until tender. Place the chickpeas in a blender or a bowl. Add the tahini, oil, garlic, salt, lemon and 4 tablespoons of warm water. Mix until creamy. If the texture is too thick, add 1-2 tablespoons of water to thin it down. Place in a serving bowl and refrigerate until needed. You may sprinkle a little paprika onto the mixture and decorate with lemon slices and black olives.

3. Raw Salads

When thinking in terms of preparing a raw salad, bear in mind that the following items can be eaten raw, either individually or as a combination. A little imagination regarding color and taste will give you a dish which will not only look attractive and taste delicious, but will provide value in the form of vitamin C and most minerals. A salad should constitute one of the main meals each day, or at least a major part of it.

The following items can be eaten raw:
Tomatoes
Onions
Scallions
Carrots
Garlic
Cauliflower
Watercress
Radishes
Radish tops (young)
Turnips, grated
Beets, grated
Parsnips, grated
Brussels sprouts
Fennel

Sea kale
Nasturtiums
Dandelions
Peas   } when young and tender
Lima beans
String beans
Cucumber
Parsley
Endive
Lettuce
Chicory
Mint
Red Cabbage
White Cabbage
Chives
Leeks
Mushrooms
Zucchini
Sprouted seeds such as:
Fenugreek
Alfalfa
Mung beans
Aduki beans
Soy beans
Lentils
Chickpeas

Chemicals seem to be used more and more in the commercial growing of vegetables and so be sure to thoroughly wash your salad ingredients before preparing the meal.

Ideally, any raw salad should be served as soon as it is prepared. In this way, such important ingredients as vitamin C will be retained instead of being lost. If, however, you have guests and wish to prepare the salad some time before the meal, then keep the prepared salad sealed in the refrigerator and add the dressing just before serving. If the dressing is added too long before serving then the salad will lose its crispness and will look "tired".

CUCUMBER SALAD
Agourosalata

(Serves 2 as a side dish)

½ a cucumber
1 large or 2 small tomatoes
4 thin slices onion
6 black olives

For the dressing:
1⅔ tablespoons oil (ideally, olive oil)
2 teaspoons cider or wine vinegar
½ teaspoon oregano
Sea salt

Wash the cucumber, tomato and onion well. Cut the cucumber in half, lengthwise, and then into slices. Cut the tomato in half and then into slices. If the tomato is large you should get 12 slices, if small, eight. Place them in a salad bowl. Add the slices of onion and olives. Mix the ingredients for the dressing thoroughly and pour this onto the salad. Mix gently but thoroughly.

TOMATO SALAD
Domatosalata

(Serves 2 as a side dish)

4 small tomatoes
⅓ green pepper
2 tablespoons finely chopped parsley
6 black olives

For the dressing:
3 tablespoons olive oil
1 teaspoon vinegar
⅓ teaspoon oregano

Wash the vegetables. Slice the tomatoes and pepper. Mix the dressing. Place the vegetables on a plate, sprinkle with parsley, pour over the dressing and decorate with the olives.

Note: The tomato slices should be generous and chunky rather than slivers. The pepper should be sliced more thinly.

CARROT AND CABBAGE SALAD
Lahano me Carota

(Serves 4 as a side dish)

½ a small white cabbage
3 carrots, coarsely grated
8 ounces canned corn, drained
3 tablespoons lemon juice
4 tablespoons olive oil
Sea salt
Dash of black pepper

Slice the cabbage *thinly*. Add to this the carrots, corn, lemon juice, olive oil and seasoning, just prior to serving. Ingredients should be well mixed.

Note: Red cabbage could be used as well and also some celery, if desired.

PEASANT SALAD
Salata Horiatiki

(Serves 2-3 as a side dish)

2-3 radishes
2 tomatoes, thinly sliced
8 slices cucumber
½ a green pepper, finely chopped
2 lettuce leaves, thinly shredded
2 scallions, thinly sliced
½ an onion, thinly sliced
4 teaspoons chopped parsley
4 teaspoons chopped mint

For the dressing:
½ teaspoon oregano
3⅓ tablespoons olive oil
4 teaspoons cider or wine vinegar
4 ounces féta or other white cheese
8 black olives

When all the salad ingredients are washed and prepared, place them in a bowl, prepare the dressing and pour it over the salad. Mix gently with a wooden serving set. Add the cheese (which should have been cut into small pieces) and the olives.

Note: This would be an ideal lunch to serve with jacket potatoes and/or wholewheat bread.

LETTUCE SALAD
Salata Marouli

(Serves 3-4 as a side dish, according to the size of the lettuce)

1 fresh, firm lettuce
4 scallions
5 mint leaves (if available) and/or
⅓ cup chopped parsley

For the dressing:
3 tablespoons olive oil
2 tablespoons lemon juice
Sea salt

Wash the salad ingredients well and tear the lettuce by hand into small pieces. Chop the scallions and mint leaves and place them in a bowl with the parsley. Add the dressing; mix thoroughly but gently and serve.

CABBAGE AND TOMATO SALAD
Salata Lahano-Domates

(Serves 4 as a side dish)

¼ small white cabbage } finely sliced and chopped
¼ small red cabbage
3 celery stalks, finely chopped
2 firm tomatoes, sliced
8 black olives

For the dressing:
3⅓ tablespoons olive oil
1⅓ tablespoons cider or wine vinegar or lemon juice
Sea salt

Place all the prepared vegetables in a bowl. Add the dressing and mix thoroughly but gently (i.e., avoid bruising the vegetables), and serve.

DANDELION, RADISH AND RADISH TOPS
Prikalida me Rapania

(Serves 2 as a side dish)

15 dandelion leaves, chopped
6 radishes and radish tops, chopped
1 small onion, sliced
8 black olives
2 small tomatoes, sliced

For the dressing:
2 tablespoons olive oil
1 tablespoon cider vinegar or lemon juice
Sea salt

Place the ingredients in a bowl; add the dressing, mix thoroughly but gently, and serve.

Note: Watercress may be added, if desired. For use in salad, the inner, tender dandelion leaves are preferable.

SALAD LETTUCE WITH EGGS
Salata Marouli me Avga

(Serves 3-4 as a side dish)

2 hard-boiled eggs
1 firm lettuce
4 scallions, chopped
A little chopped parsley and/or mint
8 black olives

For the dressing:
2⅔ tablespoons olive oil
4 teaspoons wine or cider vinegar or lemon juice
Sea salt
Freshly ground black pepper

Peel and slice the eggs. Wash all the vegetables well. In a salad bowl place the lettuce which has been hand shredded, the sliced eggs, scallions, parsley and mint. Mix the oil, vinegar, salt and pepper; add this dressing to the salad and serve.

RAW ARTICHOKE SALAD
Agginares Omes Salata

Gluten and Dairy-free
Artichokes can be eaten raw. They are very nourishing, rich in minerals and are reputed to aid liver function. They may be used raw in salad, in which case they should be prepared as described on page 60 and then diced. The rubbing of the surface with lemon is very important to delay discoloration and oxidation.

(Serves 1-2 as a side dish)

1 artichoke, diced
1 celery stalk, skinned and diced
1 tomato, sliced
6 tender dandelion leaves, chopped
2 scallions, chopped
A few olives

Dress with a generous amount of olive oil, lemon juice and a little sea salt.

4. Soups

Soups are widely used in Greece all the year round, but especially during the winter months. Soups may serve as a starter or as a main course. Frequently, a nourishing, thick vegetable soup is augmented by the addition of wholewheat pasta. This turns a simple dish into a delicious meal in itself. The wonderful range of legumes provides a large variety of choices with which to prepare soups. Red kidney beans should, if used, be boiled for at least 10 minutes prior to being added to any recipe.

The recipes given here are those I remember being prepared by my grandmother and my mother. These recipes are very easy to make, very nourishing, very tasty and very Greek.

Féta cheese, black olives and wholewheat bread (or toast) are the ideal accompaniments for any of the following soups.

POTATO SOUP

(Serves 4-5 as a starter)   *Gluten-free*

2½ pounds potatoes, peeled and diced
1 large onion, chopped
1-2 pints water (according to quality of potatoes –
    see page 16)
1½ cups goat's milk or skimmed milk
Sea salt and freshly ground black pepper
3 tablespoons polyunsaturated margarine

Place the potatoes and onion in a saucepan and cover with water. Simmer over a medium heat until the potatoes are tender. Reduce these to a creamy consistency in a food processor, then empty into a saucepan, bring to the boil and add the hot milk, salt and pepper. Stir and allow to simmer until you have a thick creamy texture. Remove from the heat and add the margarine.

LENTIL SOUP
Soupa Fakes

(Serves 4 as a main course)   *Gluten and Dairy-free*

¾ pound lentils
1 large carrot
8 cloves of garlic, halved lengthwise
½ an onion, chopped
½ teaspoon oregano
½ cup olive oil
14 ounces canned peeled tomatoes, sieved
Sea salt and black pepper to taste

Boil the lentils for 5 minutes. Empty this water and add 2 pints water; bring to the boil and allow to simmer for a further 10 minutes. Add all the other ingredients and allow to cook on a low heat until all the ingredients are tender (approximately 1 hour). When ready, the soup should be thick, but not solid. A little more water can be added, if required.

Note: This soup, eaten with wholewheat bread or toast, fresh celery and black olives is a nourishing, satisfying and extremely tasty meal in itself. This soup also freezes well.

DRIED PEA SOUP
Soupa Bizeli

(Serves 4 as a starter)   *Gluten and Dairy-free*

¾ pound dried peas
3 celery stalks, chopped
1 medium-sized onion, sliced
3 carrots, chopped
4 teaspoons polyunsaturated margarine
⅔ cup olive oil
Sea salt
Black pepper

Soak the peas overnight. Wash them well and place in a saucepan with fresh water. Simmer the peas until well cooked. In the meantime, sautée the onion with the margarine. When the onion is soft, add it to the peas and add the rest of the ingredients. Allow to simmer until the consistency is fairly thick. Blend the resulting soup into a smooth liquid prior to serving.

CHICKPEA SOUP
Soupa Revithia

(Serves 3-4 as a main course)   *Gluten and Dairy-free*

1 pound chickpeas
2 teaspoons rosemary
Sea salt
Black pepper
¾ cup olive oil
Lemon juice

Soak the chickpeas for at least 24 hours, and change the water at least twice. Simmer them for 30 minutes, then change the water; resume the cooking and change the water again 20 minutes later. Add the rosemary, salt, pepper and oil and allow to simmer until the chickpeas are *very* tender. Add a squeeze of lemon juice (according to taste), prior to serving.

BEAN SOUP
Fasoulada

(Serves 4 as a main course)   *Gluten and Dairy-free*

¾ pound navy beans
1 leek
3 carrots
2 onions   } chopped or diced
3 celery stalks
1 pound canned tomatoes
¾ cup olive oil
Sea salt
Black pepper
¼ teaspoon paprika

Soak the beans overnight. Rinse well and place in a saucepan with water. Bring to the boil and allow to cook for 15 minutes before changing the water again. Bring to the boil and allow to simmer until the beans show signs of splitting; add all the ingredients. (The tomatoes should have been passed through a sieve). Add more water if necessary and allow to simmer until the vegetables and beans are tender.

Note: The thickness of the soup is a matter of personal taste; by varying the amount of water, this can be controlled. As a winter meal, the thicker and more chewy it is, the better. Serve with olives and wholewheat bread.

TOMATO SOUP WITH SPAGHETTI
Domatosoupa me Spaghetti

(Serves 2-3 as a main course)   *Dairy-free*

1 pound canned tomatoes
2 celery stalks, chopped
1 onion, chopped
1 large carrot, chopped
½ cup olive oil
Sea salt
Black pepper
1 cupful wholewheat spaghetti, broken into
    approximately 1-inch lengths.

Place the sieved tomatoes in a saucepan. Add 3 pints of water and the celery, onion, carrot, oil, salt and pepper. Allow to simmer for 30 minutes, then add the spaghetti. Serve when the spaghetti is cooked (about 10-15 minutes).

Note: Various shapes of wholewheat pasta can be used in soups, e.g., short-cut macaroni or pasta shells. When using pasta, the resulting soup may be on the thick side. Just add some more water and another pinch of salt and bring to the boil for a minute or so before serving. Freezing any pasta soup is not recommended.

VEGETABLE SOUP
Hortosoupa

(Serves 4 as a main course)   *Gluten and Dairy-free*

1½ pounds fresh tomatoes, chopped
2 medium-sized potatoes, diced
2 carrots, diced
1 cupful red or white cabbage, finely chopped
3 celery stalks, chopped
½ cup fresh string beans, chopped
1 large onion, chopped
¾ cup olive oil
Sea salt
Black pepper

Place the tomatoes in a saucepan with 2 pints of cold water. Simmer for 30 minutes, then add all the well washed and chopped vegetables, the oil and salt and pepper and cook for approximately 45 minutes to 1 hour until the vegetables are tender.

5. Sauces

There are numerous sauces in Greek cooking, many with impressive names and even more impressive colors. Most of them, however, are meant to accompany non-vegetarian dishes. There are two basic sauces from which most others derive. These are tomato sauce and béchamel sauce.

The tomato sauce described below is the one widely used in Corfu, and it is a versatile sauce, used to accompany many pasta and rice dishes. This can be made in large quantities, as it does freeze well.

Béchamel sauce is, of course, the same the world over. I would not say its origin is Greek, but we make it "Greek style" by adding extra cheese and eggs for greater taste and nourishment. Béchamel sauce is widely used, as in moussaka dishes and Macaroni Pie, for example.

The "milk-free" béchamel, using plant milk, still contains cheese. This is usually well tolerated by individuals who are sensitive to milk itself. The soy milk used in this béchamel sauce affects the texture of the sauce, but the flavor is still delicious. It is possible that goat's cheese or cottage cheese could be used or even tofu (soy "cheese"), but the texture of the resulting sauce will obviously differ from that produced by a hard cheese. Bearing this in mind, the adventurous cook can play around with the basic ingredients and methods to produce unique creations.

TOMATO SAUCE (CORFU-STYLE)
Saltsa dae Domata

A basic ingredient of a number of dishes

Gluten and Dairy-free

3 pounds canned tomatoes (including the liquid)
1 cup parsley, chopped
1 teaspoon basil or 3 bay leaves
1 tablespoon dark brown sugar
1¼ cups olive oil
1½ large onions, chopped
⅓ cup garlic, chopped not crushed
Sea salt to taste

Place all the ingredients in a non-stick saucepan over medium heat, so that the contents are not boiling, but just gently bubbling. Stir periodically and continue for 1½ to 2 hours until all the liquid has evaporated. The result will be a thick tomato sauce.

This should be used in the preparation of vegetarian Pastitsio (Macaroni Pie), page 55, or Millet Pie, page 78 or spaghetti.

Note: Do not worry about the amount of garlic used – once cooked, most of its odor disappears. As it freezes very well you can make larger quantities for future use.

BÉCHAMEL SAUCE WITH MILK (Goat's or Cow's)
Saltza Bessamel

Quantities given in this recipe are for Macaroni, Moussaka or Millet Pies (see pages 55, 75 and 78).

   Because I consider these dishes to be a little complicated, it is better to make a larger quantity than for just one meal. Therefore, the quantities given below are intended to make 12 portions of one of these dishes, most of which can be frozen.

1½ cups wholewheat pastry flour
8 tablespoons butter or polyunsaturated margarine
3½-4 cups warm milk
1 whole egg and 5 yolks
Sea salt and freshly ground black pepper to taste
¾ pound hard cheese, grated (preferably Kefalotyri)

Place the flour and butter in a large non-stick frying pan over medium heat. Stir gently with a wooden spoon until smooth. Gradually add the milk, stirring constantly. The sauce should be thick, but not solid. (Add a little more milk if too thick.) Remove from the heat and add the egg, egg yolks, salt and pepper and cheese. Mix well and use immediately.

BECHAMEL SAUCE WITH SOY MILK
Saltsa Bessamel me Soyia

10 tablespoons wholewheat pastry flour
8 tablespoons butter or polyunsaturated margarine
1 pint soy milk ⎫
1 pint hot water ⎬ mixed together
3 whole eggs and 1 yolk
6 tablespoons grated hard cheese
Sea salt and freshly ground black pepper

Place the flour and butter in a non-stick frying pan over a medium heat. Mix to a smooth consistency and add all the milk substitute, stirring continuously. The final consistency should be thick but not solid (add a little more of the soy milk and hot water mixture if necessary). Remove from the heat and add the eggs, cheese, salt and pepper and mix well.

Note: The above quantities will make a pie or moussaka to serve 4-6, depending on what else you are serving with it.

MAYONNAISE
Mayoneza

Gluten and Dairy-free

This homemade mayonnaise contains no preservatives and should always be kept refrigerated and used within a few days of its preparation.

1 teaspoon mustard powder
1 teaspoon raw sugar
1 teaspoon sea salt
Dash of freshly ground black pepper
2 egg yolks
2 teaspoons white wine vinegar
1 cup olive oil
Juice of 1 lemon

In a bowl, mix together the mustard powder, sugar, salt and pepper. Add the egg yolks and the vinegar and mix until these and the previous ingredients are well blended. Add the oil drop by drop, stirring constantly. When the mayonnaise begins to become thick, thin it with a little lemon. Add the rest of the lemon and oil little by little until they are both fully blended. Refrigerate for 2 hours before serving.

6. Rice Dishes

Rice is a very important staple food, originating in India and brought to Europe by Alexander the Great. It is appropriate, therefore, that it should be so much a part of Greek cooking.

Whichever variety (long grain, short grain, etc.) of rice is used it is nutritionally essential to use the whole (so-called 'brown) unpolished rice and not devitalized white or polished rice. Whole rice is a valuable complex carbohydrate containing limited, but good quality protein (about 8 per cent). It also contains vitamins B_1, riboflavin (B_2), niacin and pyridoxine (B_6), in good quantities – most of these being reduced to negligible amounts by the polishing or refining process. The main mineral content of rice is potassium, magnesium and iron.

Rice is an excellent food, being easy to digest and placing little strain on the digestive system. It is particularly suitable for people with diabetic tendencies as it has been shown to be gradually absorbed (in comparison, for example, to potatoes) thus keeping the blood sugar levels stable.

Cooking instructions are difficult with rice as different varieties can require quite different timing. Rice should be rinsed in tepid water and covered in the saucepan by about 1½ inches of water. More water may be added during the cooking (in which case, carefully pour a little boiling water onto the cooking rice, trying not to disturb it). Once it is boiling, the heat should be reduced to allow a gentle simmering until all the water is absorbed. To avoid a gooey, sticky consistency, the rice should not be stirred. About 45 minutes is needed to complete the cooking process for whole rice. Cooked as described, the rice should have a fluffy quality.

As a vegetable accompaniment to a main course, a few herbs, spices or onions may be mixed with the rice prior to cooking.

Note: All rice dishes are delicious if served with plain goat's yogurt.

RICE WITH TOMATOES
Domatoryzo

(Serves 2 as a main course)   *Gluten-free*

1 large onion, chopped
2 cloves garlic, sliced not crushed
8 tablespoons polyunsaturated margrine
1 pound ripe tomatoes, chopped
2 cupsful brown rice
1 cube clear vegetable stock (from health food stores)
Sea salt
Black pepper
Grated cheese to garnish

Place the onion, garlic and margarine in a saucepan and cook until the onion is golden. Add the chopped tomatoes and allow to cook slowly over gentle heat for about 40 minutes. Add the rice and 2 to 3 cups of warm water (the quantity of water varies according to the quality of rice), and the stock, salt and pepper. Cover and allow to simmer until all the water has evaporated. Serve with the grated cheese.

Note: Wholewheat toast, tomato salad with onions, and goat's yogurt with nuts and honey as a dessert would make this a perfectly nourishing meal.

RICE WITH BUTTER AND CHEESE
Ryzi me Voutyro ke Tyri

(Serves 2 as a main course or 4-5 as a side dish) *Gluten-free*

2 cups brown rice
1 cube clear vegetable stock (from health food stores),
  dissolved in hot water
½ cup olive oil or polyunsaturated margarine
Sea salt and freshly ground black pepper
A pat of butter
Grated cheese to taste

Wash the rice well in a sieve under running tepid water.
Place the rice in a saucepan with 4-5 cups of water and the
stock. Bring to the boil. Add the olive oil, salt and pepper
and allow to simmer until all the water has evaporated, by
which time the rice should be ready (fluffy, not sticky).
Remove from the heat and add a little butter. Use a side
dish, having sprinkled grated cheese over it just prior to
serving.

BOILED RICE WITH LEMON
Rizonero me Lemoni

Gluten and Dairy-free
This recipe is widely used in Greece for medicinal purposes
– digestive upsets and diarrhea.

Brown rice
Sea salt
Olive oil
Lemon juice

Wash the rice well with tepid water. Place in a saucepan
covering it with cold water, bring to the boil and then
simmer until very soft. Make sure that all the water is
absorbed. A few minutes before removing from the heat,
add a little salt.

Quantities will, of course, vary with needs but 1 cup of
uncooked rice should make an adequate serving when
cooked. Serve the rice when no longer hot, adding 2 to 4
teaspoons olive oil and the juice of one lemon.

Note: For small quantities of rice, say ½ cup or less, use 2½
to 3 parts water to 1 part rice.

RICE WITH GOLDEN RAISINS
Ryzi me Soultanes

(Serves 2-3 as a main course)   *Gluten-free*

2 cups brown rice
½ cup olive oil or polyunsaturated margarine
1 cube clear vegetable stock
½ cup golden seedless raisins
3 scallions, chopped
½ cup sweet corn
Grated hard cheese to garnish

Prepare rice as in the recipe Rice with Butter and Cheese (page 46), omitting the grated cheese at this stage. When cooked, mix in the raisins, the chopped scallions and the corn. Grated cheese may then be added if desired. Serve hot, this makes an ideal side dish or, served cold, may be part of a salad meal. As a main course, serve with black olives, tomato salad, cheese and wholewheat toast.

Note: Using the same recipe, the corn and raisins may be replaced with peas.

RICE WITH SPINACH
Spanakoyrzo

(Serves 3-4 as a main course)   *Gluten and Dairy-free*

1 medium-sized onion, chopped
1 cup vegetable oil
3 pounds spinach, well washed and cut into large pieces
1 tablespoon tomate purée
4 cloves of garlic, sliced not crushed
2 or 3 scallions
3 tablespoons parsley
Sea salt and freshly ground black pepper
1 cup brown rice

Place the chopped onion with the oil in a wide saucepan and simmer. When the onion is golden brown, add the spinach. Continue stirring until all the spinach is lightly cooked. Then add the tomato purée to which has been added 2 cups of warm water, the garlic, scallions, parsley, salt and pepper. Allow to simmer for ¾ hour, stirring occasionally. In the meantime, precook the rice and then mix it in with the spinach. Add a little more water, if necessary, and allow to simmer until all the water has evaporated.

Note: The use of tomato is optional. If you don't use tomato though, a little lemon juice squeezed onto the dish, before serving, will improve the flavor.

LEEKS WITH RICE
Prasoryzo

(Serves 2 as a main course)   *Gluten and Dairy-free*

6 medium-sized leeks
2 pound canned tomatoes
1 cup brown rice (soaked overnight)
¼ cup olive oil
1 large onion, chopped
Sea salt and freshly ground black pepper

Clean the leeks and chop them into 1½-inch length pieces. Place these together with all the other ingredients in a saucepan. Cover (only just) with water. Simmer over a gentle heat (do not bring to the boil), until all the liquid has evaporated. Serve hot or cold.

LEEKS WITH POTATOES
Prassa me Patates

In the above recipe, the rice may be replaced by potatoes. Instead of a cup of rice add 4 medium-sized potatoes (cut into 3-4 portions each). A little less water should be used. Add a little paprika during cooking. Serve with wholewheat bread, white cheese and olives. Scallions, fresh firm tomatoes and especially watercress go well with this dish.

RICE WITH TOMATO SAUCE
Ryzi me Saltsa

Gluten-free
(As a main dish, the following quantities make 1 serving)

1 cup brown rice
¾ cup Tomato Sauce (page 40)
Grated cheese to taste

Cook the brown rice as described on page 44. Serve with the tomato sauce and a generous amount of grated cheese.

RICE CROQUETTES
Kroketes me Ryzi

(Serves several as a side dish)

1⅓ tablespoons polyunsaturated margarine
1½ cups short grain brown rice
1 cup grated hard cheese
1 small onion, grated
1½ tablespoons pine nuts
Sea salt and freshly ground black pepper
1 heaped tablespoon chopped parsley
3 eggs
12 rye crispbreads, powdered
Extra polyunsaturated margarine or vegetable oil for
    frying

In a saucepan, place 3 cups of water and 1⅓ tablespoons of margarine. Bring to the boil and add the washed rice. Stir, cover and allow to simmer until the water has completely evaporated. (If the rice is not completely cooked, add some more water and cook a little longer). Remove from the heat and add the cheese, onion, pine nuts, salt and pepper, parsley, one egg and two yolks (beat them before adding them to the mixture). Mix thoroughly and allow to stand (covered) for 30 minutes.

The rye crispbreads should be reduced to a powder with a food processor or pestle and mortar. Prepare the croquettes one by one, forming them into uniform shapes. Dip them in the rye powder, then the beaten egg whites and then again into the powder before frying in the margarine or oil. Serve hot or cold.

STUFFED ZUCCHINI WITH RICE
Kolokythakia Gemista me Ryzi

(Serves 6 as a main course)   *Gluten-free*

4 pounds medium-sized to large zucchini
1¼ pounds canned tomatoes
1 large onion, chopped
5 cloves of garlic, chopped
1½ cups olive oil
¾ cup parsley, chopped
Sea salt and freshly ground black pepper
1½ cups parboiled brown rice
½ cup grated cheese
2 tablespoons currants
¾ cup ground almonds
¼ cup pine nuts

With an instrument such as an apple corer empty the pulp of each zucchini into a saucepan, after washing them thoroughly. Add the tomatoes, onion, garlic, 1 cupful of oil, parsley, salt and pepper. Simmer until only a little liquid remains; add the rice and simmer until all the water has evaporated.

When cool, add the cheese, currants, almonds and pine nuts. Stir with a wooden spoon until all the ingredients are well mixed. Stuff the zucchini carefully with this mixture. Place them in an ovenproof container. Pour the rest of the oil over them and add salt and pepper to taste. Cook for 1 hour in a hot oven at 425°F before serving, hot or cold.

Note: Skordalia and freshly chopped salad or cold cooked vegetables (see pages 102-110) are ideal accompaniments for this traditional Greek dish, which also freezes well.

Rice is also used in the following recipes:

Lahanodolmades (Stuffed Cabbage Leaves), page 70
Dolmades (Stuffed Vine Leaves), page 72
Dolmades me Bechamel (Stuffed Vine Leaves with
     Béchamel), page 73
Agginares Moussakas (Artichoke Moussaka), page 68
Moussakas me Melitzanes (Moussaka with Eggplant),
     page 74
Melitzanes Papoutsakia (Stuffed Eggplant Papoutsakia),
     page 76

For children:

Rice, Lentils and Vegetables, page 117
Spinach, Rice, Chickpeas and Vegetables, page 120

7. Pasta Dishes

The following general advice on cooking pasta will help in the creation of delicious dishes. Wholewheat pasta is nourishing and contains the nutritional benefits of 100 percent of the grain. Typical analysis indicates around 10 percent total dietary fiber, considered important for a sound healthy digestion, 13 percent protein, as well as all the other nutrients of the whole grain. Being a minimally refined, complex carbohydrate, its value in the diet is considerable. It is also quick to prepare, inexpensive, and is enjoyed by most people.

Place the pasta (spaghetti or macaroni or any shapes such as pasta shells) in a saucepan and cover with boiling salted water. To avoid having to add more water during cooking, which can affect the quality of the final result, it is as well to be generous with the water in the first place. Once the pasta has been placed in the boiling water, it should be stirred gently to ensure that it does not stick together. When the pasta is tender (after about 15-20 minutes), remove from the heat and add 2 cups of cold water and allow to stand for half a minute. Drain in a colander before returning to the saucepan. Mix gently with 2-4 tablespoons of butter, polyunsaturated margarine or olive oil. Add a little black pepper and a small amount of grated cheese (quantities of these depend on the amount of pasta used). Wholewheat pasta may be served on its own or with wholewheat bread, black olives and a green side salad to make a perfect light meal.

When cooking pasta for children, various shapes may be used; for example, alphabet shapes, numbers or shells are often an exciting alternative to spaghetti or macaroni.

MACARONI PIE
Pastitsio

(Serves 12 – this recipe also freezes well)

Tomato Sauce (page 40)
¾ pound wholewheat macaroni (short-cut)
4 tablespoons butter
1 cup grated hard cheese
Béchamel Sauce (page 41 or 42)

Prepare the tomato sauce. Place the macaroni in boiling, slightly salted water. When cooked (after about 20 minutes), remove from the heat and add 1 quart of cold water, strain immediately through a colander. Return the cooked marcaroni to the saucepan and add the butter, grated cheese and a little pepper. Mix thoroughly but gently and cover. Prepare the béchamel sauce. Mix 1½ cups of the béchamel sauce with the macaroni. Place half of this in an ovenproof dish. Cover with a generous layer of tomato sauce and then place the remainder of the macaroni on top of this. Finally, cover with the rest of the béchamel sauce. Place in a hot oven and leave until the surface is a golden color (approximately 1 hour).

Note: This dish is delicious served hot or cold and goes well with Skordalia (page 18), broad beans and fresh salad or steamed vegetables.

MACARONI WITH BÉCHAMEL SAUCE
Macaroni me Bechamel

(Serves 12)

12 ounces wholewheat macaroni (long- or short-cut)
4 tablespoons butter
1 cup grated hard cheese
Sea salt and freshly ground black pepper
Double quantity of Béchamel Sauce (page 41 or 42)

Cook the macaroni according to the instructions given on page 54. Prepare the béchamel sauce. In a large bowl or saucepan, place the macaroni, some pepper, the butter, grated cheese, and 2 cups of the béchamel sauce. Mix these well but gently. Place half this mixture in an ovenproof dish, followed by a layer of the remaining béchamel. Then add the rest of the macaroni mixture, finishing with a layer of the remaining béchamel. Level the contents and place in a hot oven at 425°F until the surface has a golden color. Allow it to cool before cutting it into portions.

Note: This recipe should make 12 portions. What is not used can be frozen. Smaller quantities can, of course, be made by scaling down all the ingredients; however, the effort required in its preparation is doubly rewarded, not only by the pleasure the dish brings, but by having a large reserve for future use.

BAKED MACARONI
Makaronaki Cofto Sto Fourno

(Serves 4-5 as a main course)

1½ pounds very ripe fresh tomatoes
½ cup polyunsaturated margarine or butter or
   vegetable oil
4 celery stalks, chopped
Sea salt and freshly ground black pepper
1 pound wholewheat macaroni (short-cut)
Grated cheese

Peel the tomatoes (this will be made easier if the tomatoes have been placed in hot water for a few minutes). Cut them into small pieces and place in an ovenproof dish. Add the shortening or oil, celery, salt and pepper. Add 2 cups of warm water and stir. Place in a hot oven at 425°F and bake for 20 minutes. Remove from the oven and add the macaroni, stirring with a fork to make sure that it does not stick together. Return to oven. It should be ready when the water has evaporated. If the macaroni is not soft, add a little more water and cook for a little longer. Serve with a generous amount of cheese (e.g., Parmesan).

SPAGHETTI WITH TOMATO SAUCE
Spaghetti me Domata

(Serves 4-5 as a main course)

1 pound wholewheat spaghetti
Butter or polyunsaturated margarine
Sea salt and freshly ground black pepper
Tomato Sauce (page 40)
Grated hard cheese (according to taste)

Cook the spaghetti according to the instructions given on page 54. Serve with tomato sauce and a generous quantity of grated cheese (e.g., Parmesan).

SPAGHETTI WITH PEAS
Spaghetti me Bizi

(Serves 4-5 as a main course)

¾ cupful olive oil
1 medium-sized onion, chopped
2 celery stalks, chopped
½ cup parsley, chopped
1 clove of garlic, chopped
1 pound fresh peas, shelled and washed
Sea salt and freshly ground black pepper
1 pound wholewheat spaghetti
3 tablespoons butter
Grated hard cheese

Heat the olive oil in a saucepan over medium heat and add the onion, celery, parsley and garlic. Stir constantly until golden and then add the peas, salt, pepper and a cup of water. Allow to simmer over slow heat until the water has evaporated. Break the spaghetti into shorter lengths (roughly into thirds) and cook in boiling, slightly salted water. When cooked, place the saucepan under cold running water. Shake and drain through a colander. When drained, add the butter and some pepper and ½ cup of grated cheese. Mix well but gently over low heat. Add the sauce with the peas and mix carefully. Serve immediately after sprinkling with some more grated cheese.

Note: As an alternative, a little of the warmed tomato sauce may be added prior to the final grated cheese dressing.

TAGLIATELLE WITH EGGPLANT
Tayiatela me Melitzanes

(Serves 12)

Tomato Sauce (page 40)
12 ounces wholewheat tagliatelle
5 tablespoons butter, melted
1 cup grated hard cheese
2 very large or 3 medium-sized eggplants
Olive oil for frying
Béchamel Sauce (page 41 or 42)

Prepare the tomato sauce. Cook the pasta according to the instructions given on page 54. Toss gently with the butter and cheese. In the meantime, cut the eggplants lengthwise into thick slices and place them in very salty water, using sea salt. (This will draw the bitterness out of them.) Let them soak for at least 30 minutes, then dry with paper towels. Fry the slices in olive oil and place on paper towels to drain.

Prepare the béchamel sauce. In an ovenproof dish, arrange alternate layers of tagliatelle, eggplant and tomato sauce. Finish with a layer of the remaining tagliatelle before spreading the béchamel sauce on top. Place in a hot oven at 425°F, and remove when the surface is golden brown.

Note: Serve with Skordalia (page 18), steamed vegetables or fresh salad. Any remaining portions freeze well.

8. Main Meals and Side Dishes

Globe Artichokes
These are rich in vitamin A, the B vitamins and vitamin C. They contain good quantities of calcium, potassium and iron. Many health-giving properties are ascribed to artichokes, including being of use in digestive complaints, anemia and rheumatism.

In the following recipes using artichokes, the most difficult part is the preparation of the artichoke prior to cooking. Good and speedy results will be achieved if the following instructions are followed: Cut away the stem close to the head and take away most of the leaves until the tender ones are reached. Cut the artichoke into two pieces (from top to bottom) and, with a grapefruit knife, remove all the choke (hairy covering over the heart). Squeeze half a lemon into a saucepan with 1 quart cold water and, with the other half, rub the surface of the artichoke before placing it in the lemon water. This will prevent the artichokes from oxidizing and turning brown. The very tender white leaves may be included with the artichoke heart. The stem of the artichoke is also edible if the outer layer is first peeled off.

Note: For Artichokes Vinaigrette any type or shape of artichokes may be used. For all other recipes it would be preferable to obtain artichokes that are longish in shape rather than round, as these are usually more tender and easier to prepare.

Any artichoke dish tastes particularly good when served with cheese, olives and brown bread.

remove all the choke

FRIED ARTICHOKES
Agginares Tiyianites

(Use this recipe as a side dish or mezze)   *Dairy-free*

4 artichokes
1½ cups wholewheat pastry flour
1 cup warm water
1 egg
Sea salt
Olive oil for frying

Prepare the artichokes according to the instructions on page 60 and cut them in quarters if small, in eighths if large. Boil them in salty water and a little lemon juice for 10 minutes. Allow them to cool, drain them, and gently wipe them with a paper towel. Dip each piece of artichoke in a mixture of the flour and water and place into the hot oil to fry. Remove when golden. Serve hot for crispness, or cold for greater flavor.

ARTICHOKES VINAIGRETTE
Agginares Vinegrette

Gluten and Dairy-free

1 firm, well rounded artichoke per person

For the Vinaigrette:
Quantities vary according to the number of artichokes. Always use twice as much oil as vinegar. Just before serving blend the vinaigrette ingredients well.

Olive oil
Vinegar
Mustard
Sea salt
Black pepper
Raw cane sugar

Remove the stems and very small outer leaves of the artichokes. Wash well under running water, opening the leaves gently with the fingertips. Place the artichokes in a deep saucepan with plenty of slightly salted water and boil until tender (approximately 30 minutes, according to size). The artichoke is cooked when one of the central leaves can be pulled from the head with relative ease. Remove from the heat, drain and serve, warm or cold, with vinaigrette sauce.

Only the tender tip of each leaf is eaten, the leaves being removed, one by one, by hand until the heart is exposed. This part may also be eaten if the choke is first cut away. Finger bowls should be available as the process is a little oily – but delicious.

ARTICHOKES WITH POTATOES AND PEAS
Agginares me Patates Ke Bizi

(Serves 3 as a main course or 6-8 as a side dish)
Gluten and Dairy-free

4 artichokes (see preparation instructions on page 60)
1 bunch of scallions, chopped
2 cups parsley, chopped
5 cloves of garlic, chopped
1 pound frozen peas or 2 pounds fresh peas in their
   pods
2 large potatoes, peeled and cut into 5 pieces each or
6-8 small new potatoes, whole
½ cup olive oil
Sea salt
Black pepper

When all the vegetables are washed, place them in a large non-stick saucepan. Add the olive oil, salt and pepper and cover with water. Simmer over medium heat, stirring gently from time to time until the warm water has evaporated. Serve hot or warm.

Note: If served as a main course, serve with cottage or féta cheese, wholewheat bread and olives. Skordalia would also complement this dish.

COOKED ARTICHOKE SALAD
Agginares Salata

Gluten and Dairy-free
This is a side dish to accompany any main dish. Quantities of ingredients depend upon the number of servings required.

Artichokes
Onion juice
Tomatoes
Boiled potatoes ⎫
Hard-boiled eggs ⎬   optional
Salad dressing ⎭

For the Salad Dressing:
Lemon juice ⎱
Olive oil   ⎰ Use twice as much oil as lemon juice
Sea salt
Black pepper

For this recipe small young artichokes, cooked whole, are ideal; if large, see the instructions for preparation on page 60. Boil the washed and trimmed artichokes in lightly salted water until tender. Drain, allow to cool and then cut into small pieces (about ½-inch cubes), and place in a salad bowl. Add a few drops of onion juice, if liked, the sliced tomatoes, boiled potatoes and hard-boiled eggs. Pour a dressing of oil and lemon juice over the salad.

ARTICHOKES À LA POLITA
Agginares à la Polita

(Serves 4 as a main course)   *Dairy-free*

4 large artichokes
8 new potatoes, scrubbed and left whole
6 small onions, peeled and left whole
2 medium-sized carrots, sliced
8 scallions, chopped
1 cup olive oil
Juice of 1 lemon
1½ cups parsley, chopped
1 cup fresh dill, if available
Sea salt
Black pepper
1 tablespoon wholewheat pastry flour

Prepare the artichokes according to the instructions on page 60. Place in a saucepan and add the potatoes, the whole onions, sliced carrots, scallions, olive oil, lemon juice, parsley, dill, salt and pepper. Mix the flour with a cup of water and add to the above ingredients. Cover with warm water and allow to simmer over medium heat, uncovered, for approximately 1 hour. When all the water has evaporated, the ingredients should be ready. Remove from the heat and place a double piece of parchment paper between the lid and the saucepan (being careful not to touch the contents). This will absorb the steam, when removed from the heat, prior to serving.

Note: Serve with cottage cheese (or, ideally, féta), wholewheat bread and black olives.

ARTICHOKES WITH BROAD BEANS
Agginares me Koukia

(Serves 4 as a main course)   *Gluten and Dairy-free*

6 artichokes
2½ pounds broad beans
8 whole new potatoes or
2 large old potatoes, cut into 4 pieces each (scrubbed if
    new, peeled if old)
1 bunch of scallions, chopped
4 cloves of garlic, chopped
1½ cups parsley, chopped, and fresh dill
    (if no dill available, just use parsley)
⅔ cup olive oil
Sea salt
Black pepper

Prepare the artichokes according to the instructions on page 60. To prepare the broad beans, remove the shells if they are large ones, but for any small tender ones, use the shells as well, having removed any stringy fibers. Place all the ingredients in a non-stick saucepan; only just cover with water. Allow to simmer over medium heat until all the water has evaporated (approximately 1½ hours).

Remove from the heat and place parchment paper between the saucepan and the lid. This will absorb the steam. Allow to stand until ready to serve, hot or cold. Serve with cheese, wholewheat bread and black olives.

ARTICHOKES WITH BÉCHAMEL SAUCE
Agginares me Saltsa Bechamel

(Serves 4 as a main course)

8-10 artichokes
Juice of 1 lemon
½ cup polyunsaturated margarine or butter, melted
Sea salt
Black pepper
Béchamel Sauce (page 41 or 42)
2 cups grated hard cheese
Wholewheat breadcrumbs

Prepare the artichokes according to the instructions on page 60. Place them in a saucepan with boiling water to which has been added a little salt and the lemon juice. Cover and simmer for no more than 10 minutes. Drain and allow to cool. Dice the artichokes and sauté gently with half of the margarine or butter and add salt and pepper to taste.

Prepare the béchamel sauce. Into an ovenproof dish pour a layer of the sauce and sprinkle this with half each the grated cheese and breadcrumbs. Then place a layer of the diced artichokes, also sprinkled with cheese and breadcrumbs. Cover this with the remainder of the béchamel; level the surface and carefully sprinkle the rest of the cheese on top. Pour the rest of the margarine or butter onto the surface. Place in a pre-heated hot oven at 425°F and remove when golden.

Note: Serve this meal with lima beans, potato salad and steamed zucchini. Cottage cheese and olives would also go well with it.

ARTICHOKE MOUSSAKA
Agginares Moussakas

(Serves 12)

8 artichokes
14 ounces canned tomatoes
1 large onion, chopped
½ cup chopped parsley
3 cloves of garlic, chopped
¾ cup olive oil
2 bay leaves or ⅓ teaspoon dried basil
Sea salt
Black pepper
2¼ cups long grain brown rice, cooked
½ cup sunflower seeds and/or pine nuts or ground
    almonds
1 tablespoon raisins
Béchamel Sauce (page 41 or 42)

Prepare the artichokes in the usual way (see page 60). Boil them in lightly salted water for 10 minutes. Drain, allow to cool and cut into slices. In a non-stick saucepan, heat the tomatoes, having added the onion, chopped parsley, garlic, oil, bay leaves, salt and pepper. Allow to simmer until all the water has evaporated.

Remove from the heat. Add the rice which should have been pre-cooked in water with a little salt added. Remove the bay leaves. Add to this mixture the sunflower seeds and the raisins. Mix well. In an ovenproof dish, place a layer of sliced artichokes and then cover with all the contents of the tomato-rice mixture. Level this out before placing the remaining sliced artichokes on top.

Prepare the béchamel sauce. Cover the dish with a generous layer of this and place in a 425°F oven until the surface is golden brown.

Note: The moussaka may be started with a layer of potato slices (simply boil and slice several large potatoes in advance). Also, for extra nourishment, 2 tablespoons of grated cheese may be added to the rice mixture. This dish should be accompanied by steamed vegetables (carrots and peas), and/or potato and beet salad, wholewheat bread and olives.

JERUSALEM ARTICHOKES WITH TOMATOES
Karkiofoles me Domato

(Serves 2-3 as a side dish)   *Gluten and Dairy-free*

1 pound Jerusalem artichokes
8 ounces canned whole tomatoes
¾ cup parsley and/or fresh dill, chopped
Sea salt
Black pepper
½ teaspoon dark brown sugar
8 scallions, chopped
3-4 cloves of garlic, chopped
½ cup olive oil

Scrub the artichokes to remove any dirt and soil. If they are large, cut in two to three pieces, otherwise cook them whole. Put all the ingredients, except the artichokes, into a non-stick saucepan. Add 1 cup of water and bring to the boil. When half of the liquid has evaporated, add the artichokes. Partially cover and simmer until all the water has evaporated.

Note: This side dish can be served with any meal.

STUFFED CABBAGE LEAVES
Lahanodolmades

(Serves 4 as a main course)

1 cup brown rice
1 tablespoon currants
4 scallions, chopped
2 teaspoons pine nuts, if available
Sea salt and pepper
2⅔ tablespoons olive oil
1 egg white
2 teaspoons ground almonds
1 tablespoon grated cheese
2 tablespoons chopped parsley
1 large Savoy cabbage
1 cup lemon juice

For the sauce:
3⅓ tablespoons wholewheat pastry flour
4 tablespoons butter
2 cups milk
2 egg yolks
2 tablespoons grated hard cheese

Boil the rice for about 8 minutes. Strain and place in a mixing bowl. Add the currants, scallions, pine nuts, salt, pepper, half the oil, the egg white (lightly beaten), the almonds, grated cheese and parsley. Mix to blend well.

Boil the cabbage for 2-3 minutes to soften the outer leaves. Separate the cabbage leaves and place about a tablespoon of the stuffing in the center of each leaf, folding to enclose the mixture. Place the envelope in a non-stick saucepan. When the stuffing has all been used, chop any remaining leaves and spread on top of the stuffed leaves. Place two small plates over the leaves (this is to keep the contents firmly in place). Add the remaining olive oil, salt, pepper and the lemon juice and enough water to cover the contents of the saucepan. Simmer very gently over medium-low heat for 30 to 40 minutes until, by tipping the saucepan, you can see only about a cup of liquid remaining. Remove from the heat and remove the plates covering the cabbage.

Prepare the sauce as follows:
Pour the remaining liquid from above into a cup. Place the flour and butter together in a frying pan on medium heat. Stir continuously until these are all well mixed. Add, alternately, a little milk and cabbage water, until these are used, stirring continuously. Remove the pan from the heat. Add the two egg yolks and mix well and then add the cheese and a touch of salt and pepper. Pour this sauce into the saucepan containing the stuffed leaves. Encourage this to permeate between the stuffed cabbage leaves by shaking the container fairly vigorously. Bring back to the boil for half a minute. Remove and serve. This is delicious hot or cold, and also freezes well.

Note: This dish tastes particularly good with Skordalia (page 18), potatoes and steamed zucchini or beans.

JERUSALEM ARTICHOKES WITH PEAS
Karkiofoles me Bizi

(Serves 2-3 as a side dish)   *Gluten and Dairy-free*

1 pound Jerusalem artichokes
1 10-ounce carton frozen peas
¾ cup parsley, chopped
Sea salt
Black pepper
8 scallions, chopped
3-4 cloves of garlic, chopped
½ cup olive oil

Scrub the artichokes to remove any dirt and soil. If they are large, cut in two to three pieces, otherwise cook them whole. Put the ingredients, except artichokes and peas, into a non-stick pan. Add 1 cup of warm water and bring to the boil. When half of the liquid has evaporated add the artichokes and the peas. Partially cover and simmer until all the water has evaporated.

STUFFED VINE LEAVES
Dolmades

(Serves 4-6)   *Gluten-free*

1 onion, chopped
¾ cup olive oil
1½ cups long grain brown rice
4 teaspoonsful dill and/or parsley
2 scallions, chopped
Sea salt and freshly ground black pepper
½ cup currants
½ cup pine nuts or ground almonds
1 egg white
50 vine leaves
Juice of 1½ lemons

Place the onion in a saucepan with half of the oil over medium heat. Stir the onion until only very light brown and then remove from the heat. In the meantime, boil the rice in slightly salted water for 10 minutes before draining and adding it to the onion. Add the dill, the scallions, salt and pepper, 2 teaspoons of the olive oil, the currants, pine nuts and the egg white. Mix them gently together.

To prepare the vine leaves:
If picked from the garden, pick tender but good-sized leaves. Wash them well and remove the stems with scissors. Boil the leaves in salted water for 15 minutes. Drain and place on a clean surface to cool. If the leaves are shop bought, then rinse well and boil in plain water for 15 minutes.

Cover the bottom of a non-stick saucepan with a layer of leaves. Then take the leaves one by one, placing 2 teaspoons of the mixture onto each, before folding carefully into an envelope shape. Place these in the saucepan. When all the leaves have been used, pour the lemon juice and the rest of the olive oil over them. Add a touch of salt and pepper, and before covering with warm water, place one or two plates over them to keep the piles of stuffed vine leaves in place during the cooking process.

Cook over medium heat until the water evaporates; remove from the heat, remove the plates and allow to cool for about 10 minutes. Then gently place the stuffed vine leaves on a serving dish. These may be served hot or cold.

Note: If served hot, they may be accompanied by Hummus (page 23) or Skordalia (page 18), lima beans and other steamed vegetables. If served cold, Tjatjiki (page 20) or even plain goat's yogurt, with any fresh salad would be an ideal accompaniment.

STUFFED VINE LEAVES WITH BÉCHAMEL
Dolmades me Bechamel

Prepare the vine leaves exactly as in the previous recipe for Stuffed Vine Leaves. Ensure that there is one teacupful of liquid left from the cooking process. Then prepare the Béchamel Sauce as follows:

3⅓ tablespoons wholewheat pastry flour
4 tablespoons butter
2 cups milk (cow's, goat's or soy)
2 egg yolks
1⅓ tablespoons grated hard cheese (optional)
Sea salt and freshly ground pepper

Put the flour and butter together in a frying pan and place over a medium heat. Stir continuously until well mixed. Add, alternately, a little milk and a little liquid from cooking the vine leaves, until all is used up – stirring all the time. Remove the pan from the heat. Add the two egg yolks and mix well, then add the cheese and a touch of salt and pepper.

Pour this sauce into the saucepan containing the stuffed vine leaves, and encourage it to permeate the vine leaves by shaking the container fairly vigorously.

Bring back to the boil for half a minute. Remove from heat and serve. This is delicious hot or cold.

MOUSSAKA WITH EGGPLANT
Moussakas me Melitzanes

This is a traditional dish. In Greece it is cooked with minced meat, which I have replaced with brown rice, a little grated cheese, currants and seeds for taste and nourishment. Many people who eat meat, after sampling this recipe have preferred it to the orthodox one.

(Serves 8-12) (dimension of container 10 in. x 12 in. and 2 in. depth)

3-4 large eggplants
Olive oil for frying
1¼ cups short-grain brown rice
1 pound canned tomatoes
1 large onion, chopped
3 tablespoons chopped parsley
½ cup olive oil
3 cloves of garlic, chopped
Sea salt and freshly ground pepper
2 tablespoons sunflower seeds
3 tablespoons pine nuts and/or
½ cupful currants
3 tablespoons grated cheese
Béchamel Sauce (page 41 or 42)

Cut each eggplant lengthwise into slices (just under half an inch thick). Place these in a container with plenty of water and sea salt – 1 teaspoon of sea salt to 1 pint of water. Allow them to soak for a minimum of 30 minutes to remove the bitter juices. Rinse well, dry with paper towels and then fry in olive oil.

Wash the rice well, cover by about 1½ inches of cold water and simmer for 20 minutes. Add the tomatoes, with their juice (having first sliced the tomatoes with a sharp knife); also add the onion and parsley, the olive oil and garlic, salt and pepper. Bring to the boil and simmer, stirring occasionally. When all the water has evaporated, remove from the heat and add the seeds, pine nuts, currants and the grated cheese.

Make the béchamel sauce according to the instructions

on page 41 or 42. Take one eggplant at a time and form a layer in the ovenproof container with half of them. (They should cover the surface). The second layer should then be made with the rice mixture. Spread it gently and evenly. With the remaining eggplant, make another layer on top of the rice. Finally spread a thick layer of béchamel evenly on the top. Place in a 425°F oven and cook until the surface turns golden brown. Allow it to cool before cutting into portions.

Note: The color of the sliced eggplant might change to brown but this does not affect the taste. This dish also freezes well.

MOUSSAKA WITH POTATOES AND ZUCCHINI
Moussakas me Patates ke Kolokithia

Ingredients as on page 74, replacing eggplants with potatoes and zucchini.
   The method of preparing the dish is the same as for the Moussaka with Eggplant. Simply replace the eggplants with 4 large potatoes washed well, sliced and fried (cut them into circular slices), and 6 zucchini, cut lengthwise and also fried. The bottom layer must be made with potatoes, followed by the rice, then the zucchini and finally the béchamel.

MOUSSAKA WITH POTATOES
Moussakas me Patates

Prepare in the same way as Moussaka with Eggplant (page 74). Replace the eggplants with 3 pounds potatoes, cut into circular slices and fried. Cover the surface of an ovenproof container with a little oil, as the potatoes might stick. In the container form a bottom layer of potatoes, followed by the rice mixture, a second layer of potatoes and then the béchamel sauce.

Note: Either dish can be served with Skordalia and lima beans, and does freeze well.

STUFFED EGGPLANT PAPOUTSAKIA
Melitzanes Papoutsakia ('Little Shoes')

(Serves 4 as a main course)

8 small eggplants
1¾ cups short-grain brown rice
2 cups canned tomatoes
1 large Spanish onion, chopped
4 cloves of garlic, chopped
½ cup chopped parsley
¾ cup olive oil
3-4 tablespoons pine nuts and/or sunflower seeds or
   ground almonds
Sea salt and freshly ground black pepper
2 tablespoons currants
3 tablespoons grated cheese
Béchamel Sauce (page 41 or 42)

Remove a thin lengthwise section from each eggplant. Gently, with the help of a grapefruit knife and a small spoon, scrape out the flesh. Allow the empty eggplants to soak for up to 30 minutes in salted water. In the meantime, wash the rice and place it in a saucepan covered with 1½ cups of cold water. Simmer for 20 minutes and then add the tomatoes with their juice. Add the eggplant flesh, the onion, garlic, parsley, olive oil, salt and pepper. Bring to the boil and simmer for approximately 1 hour, stirring occasionally. When all the water has evaporated, remove from the heat and add the pine nuts, seeds, currants and the grated cheese and mix well.

Boil the eggplant shells in slightly salted water for 5 minutes. Drain, season the inside with a little pepper, and then stuff them with the mixture. Place in an ovenproof casserole.

Prepare the béchamel sauce, half the quantity given on page 41. Divide it on top of each stuffed eggplant. Place in a hot oven 425°F until the béchamel is golden brown. Serve with Skordalia and steamed vegetables.

Note: This dish can be prepared without béchamel, in which case, replace the section previously removed, season and pour a few drops of olive oil on top of each eggplant. Cook in the oven for approximately 1 hour. It also freezes well.

LENTIL AND NUT LOAF
Fakes me Amygdala Lefti

(**Serves 6-8**) *Dairy-free*

8 ounces lentils
1 large onion, chopped
8 cloves of garlic, whole
3 tablespoons olive oil
1 cup ground walnuts or almonds and/or pine nuts
3 cups wholewheat breadcrumbs
2 tablespoons tomato purée
1½ teaspoons oregano
3 tablespoons chopped parsley
2 eggs
Sea salt and freshly ground black pepper

To serve:
Garnish with tomato, onion, parsley

Soak the lentils for several hours, rinse, place in a saucepan and cover with cold water. Simmer gently for 20 minutes, by which time they should be tender. Any surplus liquid should be drained. Fry the onion and garlic in oil in a large saucepan until lightly brown. Remove from the heat and add the nuts, lentils, breadcrumbs, tomato purée, oregano, parsley and eggs. After mixing well, season with salt and pepper.

Place a strip of foil on the bottom and up the sides of a loaf pan. Grease it with butter. Place the mixture in the loaf pan and cover it with greased foil. Bake in the oven at 350°F for about 1 hour. After removing from the oven, leave the loaf in the pan for a few minutes. Run a knife around the edge of the pan and turn out the loaf. Serve in thick slices with salad or a cooked vegetable salad (page 106).

MILLET PIE
Korakiana

This is a nourishing and extremely tasty dish. It has a high protein content and is rich in minerals such as calcium, iron, phosphorus and most of the B-complex vitamins. The recipe provides 12 good portions which can be individually stored in a freezer. Portions should be defrosted at room temperature. If placed in an oven to warm, prior to serving, cover with foil to avoid dryness. Ideally, serve with lima beans or lentils as a side dish as well as steamed vegetables or with a raw salad.

(Serves 12)

2½ cups millet
5 cups water
2 vegetable bouillon cubes
½ large or 1 small onion, chopped
5-6 scallions, chopped
¾ cup parsley, chopped
½ cup pine nuts and/or
½ cup almonds, peeled and ground
¾ cup golden raisins
5 heaped tablespoons butter or polyunsaturated
　　margarine
Sea salt and freshly ground black pepper
Tomato Sauce (page 40)
Béchamel Sauce (page 41 or 42)

Add the millet to boiling salted water containing the bouillon cubes. Simmer until the millet is tender, by which time all the water should have evaporated. Add all the remaining ingredients except the sauces and mix well, having removed the saucepan from the heat. Place half of the mixture in an ovenproof container and cover with the tomato sauce. Add the rest of the millet mixture and pour the béchamel sauce over the top. Place in a preheated, very hot oven at 450°F and cook until the surface is golden brown, about 1 hour.

Note: Using the same method, individual pies can be

prepared in ovenproof containers. These can also be frozen or served direct from the oven.

STUFFED SQUASH BLOSSOMS
Kolokytholoulouda Gemista

(Serves 2 as a side dish)

16 squash blossoms
½ cup cottage cheese or féta cheese
1 egg
2 scallions, finely chopped
1⅓ tablespoons chopped parsley (optional)
Sea salt and freshly ground black pepper
Vegetable oil for frying (preferably olive oil)

For the batter:
Mix thoroughly 1½ cups wholewheat pastry flour, 1 cup of water, 1 egg, a little sea salt and 1 tablespoon of olive oil

Wash the flowers very gently as they are fragile, taking care not to break them. Mix the cheese (having removed some of its liquid by gently squeezing it in cheesecloth or a kitchen towel), with the beaten egg, the scallions, parsley, salt and pepper. Put a spoonful of the mixture in each flower, dip in the batter and fry in hot oil until golden. Serve this delicacy hot or cold as an appetizer or side dish.

WHOLE MUSHROOMS PLAIN
Oloklira Manitaria Sketa

(Serves 3-4 as a side dish)   *Gluten-free*

1 pound button mushrooms
2 tablespoons butter or polyunsaturated margarine or
   ½ cup olive oil
Sea salt and freshly ground black pepper

Wash the mushrooms well and place them in a saucepan, together with the butter or oil, sea salt and pepper. Simmer on a medium to low heat for 20 minutes. At this stage, turn the heat high and stir constantly until all the liquid has evaporated. Serve warm.

Note: Non-button mushrooms can be cooked in the same way. With button mushrooms, however, freshness can be ensured with more tasty results.

MUSHROOMS WITH TOMATOES
Manitaria me Domata

(Serves 3-4 as a side dish)   *Gluten-free*

1 pound canned tomatoes or 5 fresh tomatoes
2 tablespoons butter or ½ cup olive oil
1 large Spanish onion, finely chopped
Sea salt and freshly ground black pepper
1 pound button mushrooms

In a saucepan, place the tomatoes which have been finely chopped (if canned tomatoes are used add the juice, if fresh tomatoes are used, add 1 cup of water), the butter or oil, the onion, sea salt and pepper. Bring to the boil and simmer (covered) for 20 minutes. Then add the well washed and sliced mushrooms. Cover and simmer for a further 15-20 minutes and then uncover the saucepan, turn the heat up to maximum and stir constantly until all the liquid has evaporated. Serve warm.

MUSHROOMS IN BUTTER A LA FLOSSI
Manitaria me Voutyro

(Serves 3-4 as a side dish)   *Gluten-free*

1 pound button mushrooms
1 large Spanish onion, chopped
2-3 small carrots, sliced
Sea salt and freshly ground black pepper
2 tablespoons butter

Wash the mushrooms thoroughly and slice them across into two, three or four slices (according to mushroom size). Add the onion, carrots, salt, pepper and butter to the saucepan. Place on a medium heat (add no water) and simmer for approximately 20 minutes, stirring occasionally. Then turn the heat full on, stirring constantly until all the juice has evaporated. Serve warm.

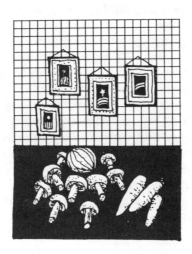

STUFFED TOMATOES WITH EGGS
Domates Gemistes me Ayga

(Serves 2 as a main course)

1 pound new potatoes
4 very large tomatoes
Sea salt and freshly ground black pepper
8 ounces hard cheese
¼ cup chopped parsley
1 cup olive oil
4 eggs
2 teaspoons powdered whole-rye crispbread
1¼ cups brown rice
2 teaspoons butter or polyunsaturated margarine

Scrub the potatoes well, removing all the skin and then boil for 20 minutes. Wash the tomatoes well, remove the tops and carefully scoop out the pulp. Season the inside of each tomato and place in the ovenproof container, preferably pyrex.

Before grating the cheese, cut four thin slices to be kept on one side. Put the half-cooked potatoes around the tomatoes in the ovenproof container. Put a pinch of parsley, some grated cheese and half a teaspoon of olive oil into each tomato. Purée the pulp of the tomatoes. Season and add the parsley and the rest of the olive oil. Mix well and pour this over the potatoes. Bake in a moderately hot oven, 375°F, for 35 minutes. Remove and place a slice of the cheese in each tomato. Break the eggs and carefully pour one into each tomato. Season the eggs and add the rye crispbread crumbs. Finally, with a spoon, pour some of the liquid from the ovenproof container onto the potatoes and onto each egg. Place back in the oven and bake for a further 20-30 minutes.

Boil the rice in salted water. When ready, add the butter and a pinch of freshly ground black pepper. Serve 2 tomatoes on each plate and surround with the potatoes and rice. Dress the rice with the remaining juice and sprinkle grated cheese over the top.

TOMATOES STUFFED WITH MAYONNAISE
Domates Gemistes me Mayoneza

(Serves 4 as a side dish or starter)   *Gluten and Dairy-free*

8 small tomatoes
Sea salt and freshly ground black pepper
½ cup diced cucumber
1 medium-sized zucchini, boiled and diced
1 medium-sized potato, boiled and diced
Mayonnaise (page 43)
8 black olives
⅓ cup chopped parsley

Select small and very firm tomatoes. Cut a slice from the top and scrape out the pulp. Season the empty tomatoes with the salt and pepper, turn them upside-down and allow them to drain for about 1 hour. In a bowl, mix the diced cucumber, zucchini, potato and a little of the tomato flesh (having first removed the seeds). Season and add 1 or 2 tablespoons of the mayonnaise. Stuff the tomatoes with this mixture. Finish with a teaspoon of mayonnaise on top of each tomato. Decorate with a black olive in the middle surrounded by the freshly chopped parsley. (If parsley is not available, chopped watercress can be used.) When ready, refrigerate and serve cold.

Note: Ideally, this dish is used as a starter on a warm summer's day.

MIXED GRILLED VEGETABLES
Lahanika sti Shara

(Serves 1 as a side dish)

1 large tomato
1 large clove of garlic, crushed
1 spoon parsley, finely chopped
1 tablespoon polyunsaturated margarine
Pinch of oregano
Sea salt and freshly ground black pepper
2 large mushrooms
1 small onion, cut in half

Cut the tomato in half. Gently empty the pulp with a spoon into a bowl. Cut the tomato flesh into small pieces. Add the crushed garlic, parsley, half of the margarine, the oregano and a little salt and pepper. Mix well and refill the empty tomato halves with the mixture.

Wash the mushrooms and onion well, sprinkle with salt and pepper and add a little of the remaining margarine. Place these and the tomato under the broiler until the tomatoes are slightly brown. Serve hot.

PIES

Pies are traditionally made with very fine pastry called "fyllo", which is as thin as rice paper and made with very fine white flour. To make this as a wholefood is impossible since brown wholewheat flour cannot be reduced to the thinness of cigarette paper. The taste though, and the nourishment are found in the pie contents which, in the following recipes, are described in the traditional way. I have only changed the dishes by describing them as being made with wholewheat flour rather than the more easily prepared, ready-made fyllo.

When fyllo is used, several layers are placed on the bottom of the ovenproof container, each one being brushed with a little butter or margarine, using a pastry brush. The mixture is then put in, followed by more buttered layers of fyllo before the dish is baked in the oven. Ready-made fyllo can be bought in gourmet food shops; however, for wholefood cooking, the short crust pastry recipe (below) should be used.

SHORT CRUST PASTRY

2 cups wholewheat flour
Pinch of salt
4 tablespoons nut butter (from health food stores)
1-2 tablespoons butter or polyunsaturated margarine
Cold water to mix

Sieve the flour and salt together and rub the fat into the flour until the mixture looks like breadcrumbs, then add enough cold water to make a stiff dough (about ½ cup of cold water). Roll out with a floured rolling pin (or floured bottle if no rolling pin is available) to about ¼ inch thick.

The above quantities will make 2 layers of short crust pastry for an 8-inch diameter container (this would serve 4 portions as a main course). Greater quantities could be useful, as all the following pie recipes freeze well.

SPINACH PIE
Spanakopita

1 pound spinach
2 tablespoons polyunsaturated margarine or butter
½ small onion, chopped
2 scallions, chopped
2 cloves of garlic, chopped
⅓ cup chopped dill
⅓ cup chopped parsley
Sea salt and freshly ground black pepper
2 eggs
8 ounces white cheese (féta or cottage cheese)
⅓ cup milk
Short crust pastry (page 85)

Wash the spinach well and cut into small pieces. Put the margarine into a frying pan together with the onion, scallions, garlic, dill and parsley and sauté until they begin to soften. Then add the spinach, salt and pepper and allow to cook uncovered until all the liquid produced by the spinach has evaporated. Remove from the heat and allow to cool.

In another bowl, beat the eggs. Add a little salt and pepper and when well beaten, add the cheese. If féta is used, crumble the cheese. If cottage cheese is used, first place on paper towels to remove excess liquid before adding the cheese to the beaten eggs. Add the milk, mix well and then add to the spinach. Mix thoroughly and test for seasoning.

Line a buttered pie plate (about 2 inches deep) with a layer of the short crust pastry and then empty all the spinach mixture into it. Level this and cover with the remaining layer of pastry. Score the surface to mark the portions. This facilitates serving when cooked. Place in a medium to hot oven at 375°F until the pastry looks brown (about 30-40 minutes). Serve hot or at room temperature.

LEEK PIE
Prasopita

(Serves 4 as a main meal)

3-4 medium-sized leeks
⅓ cup polyunsaturated margarine or butter
2 eggs
1 cup cottage cheese or féta, crumbled
Sea salt and freshly ground black pepper
2 tablespoons powdered rye crispbread
Short crust pastry (page 85)

Wash and chop the leeks coarsely. In a frying pan, place the margarine and the leeks. Sauté over low heat with no cover until all the liquid has evaporated.

In the meantime, beat the eggs, add the cheese (if féta is used, crumble, if cottage cheese, then place it for a while on paper towels to remove surplus moisture). Add the egg-cheese mixture to the leeks, together with some salt and pepper and the powdered rye crispbread.

Line a buttered 8-inch pie plate with the short crust pastry. Empty the leek mixture into it and cover with the remaining pastry. Mark the surface with a knife to facilitate cutting into sections when serving, and bake in a medium to hot oven at 375°F. Remove when the surface is golden brown and serve hot.

CHEESE PIE
Tyropita

(Serves 9-12 as a main course)

Short crust pastry (page 85)
1¼ pound féta cheese, crumbled
1 cup parsley, finely chopped, and/or dill
Béchamel Sauce

For the bechamel sauce:
3⅓ tablespoons butter
7 tablespoons wholewheat pastry flour
3 cups milk
Sea salt and freshly ground black pepper
6 eggs

Prepare the short crust pastry for an ovenproof pie dish with dimensions 12 in. x 10 in. x 2 in. For this, approximately four times the quantities given on page 85 will be required.

In a large bowl, crumble the cheese. In the meantime, melt the butter in a frying pan and add the flour. Stirring constantly, add the milk a little at a time; add some salt and pepper (if the sauce is too thick add a little more milk). Allow to cool and add this to the cheese together with the herbs. Beat the eggs lightly and combine them with the other ingredients. Line the pie dish with pastry and then empty all the cheese-béchamel-egg mixture into the pie dish and level out. Cover with the remaining pastry. Mark the surface with a sharp knife to facilitate cutting into portions when serving. Place in a medium to hot oven at 375°F. Remove when the surface is golden brown and serve warm or cold. This pie also freezes well.

FOODS WITII OLIVE OIL
Lathera Fagita

This type of food is widely used in Greece and particularly during the spring and summer. Such dishes can be used as appetizers or as main courses. If used as a main course, then it should be accompanied by fresh wholewheat bread, féta cheese and a small tomato-cucumber salad.

The use of garlic in many of these dishes enhances the ability of the body to digest the oil. Serve hot or cold.

STEWED ZUCCHINI
Kolokythia Lathera

(Serves 3-4 as a side dish)

1 large onion, finely chopped
¾ cup olive oil
¾ cup canned tomatoes
½ cup finely chopped parsley
5 cloves of garlic
Sea salt and freshly ground black pepper
3 pounds medium-sized zucchini

Place the onion and oil in a saucepan. Heat and stir until the onion is slightly discolored. Add the tomatoes, parsley, garlic, salt, pepper and a cup of warm water. Allow to simmer until the sauce slightly thickens and then add the zucchini which, in the meantime, have been washed and cut into 3-4 large pieces each. Simmer until all the water has evaporated and serve hot or cold. This dish freezes well.

CAULIFLOWER STEW
Kounoupidi Stifado

This very popular Greek side dish is cooked in tomatoes and spices.

(Serves 4-6 as a side dish)   *Gluten and Dairy-free*

1 large onion, chopped
4 cloves of garlic, coarsely chopped
¾ cup olive oil
1 pound canned tomatoes
Sea salt and freshly ground black pepper
4 bay leaves
⅔ teaspoon rosemary
10 very small onions, whole
1 large or 2 medium-sized cauliflowers
3 tablespoons wine vinegar

Place the chopped onion and garlic with the olive oil in a saucepan (preferably non-stick), and cook, stirring constantly, until the onion is lightly browned. Add the tomatoes with their juice to the onions, together with salt and pepper, the bay leaves (bruised for extra flavor) and the rosemary. Add a cup of warm water and simmer for 20 minutes. Add the small whole onions, stir and simmer for a further 15 minutes. Then add the cauliflower which should, in the meantime, have been washed, detached from its leaves and cut into large pieces. Add another ½ cup of warm water, stir gently and allow to simmer until the water has evaporated. Add the wine vinegar, stir gently and simmer for a further 3-4 minutes on a gentle heat. Remove from the heat. The result should be a slightly undercooked cauliflower in a thick tomato and onion sauce.

Note: Serve hot or at room temperature. Remove the bay leaves before serving.

CORFU ONIONS WITH TOMATOES
Kremydia Stifado

(Serves 3-4 as a side dish)   *Gluten and Dairy-free*

1 large Spanish onion, chopped
½ cup olive oil
8 ounces canned tomatoes
4 bay leaves
½ teaspoon paprika
3 cloves of garlic, sliced
Sea salt and freshly ground black pepper
16-20 small onions, whole
2 tablespoons wine or cider vinegar

Place the chopped onion in a non-stick saucepan with the olive and cook until the onion becomes slightly brown. Add the tomatoes (cut into small segments), the bay leaves (bruised), paprika, garlic, salt, pepper and half a cup of warm water. Allow the mixture to simmer for 20 minutes, stirring occasionally. Then add the whole onions. Cover and simmer gently until all the water evaporates, leaving the onions in a thick sauce. Five minutes before removing from the heat, add the vinegar. Serve warm or at room temperature.

OVEN-BAKED EGGPLANT WITH HERBS
Melitzanes Fournou

(Serves 4 as a side dish)   *Gluten and Dairy-free*

½ cup olive oil
1 large onion, chopped
4 cloves of garlic, chopped
⅓ cup white wine
1 pound canned tomatoes
¾ cup parsley, finely chopped
1-2 bay leaves, fresh or dried
Sea salt and freshly ground black pepper
1 tablespoon raw cane sugar
2 large eggplants

Place the olive oil in a large non-stick saucepan or a deep frying pan. Add the onion and garlic. Stir constantly over medium heat until the onion is slightly golden. Add the wine and stir for a few more minutes. Then add the tomatoes, parsley, bay leaves, salt, pepper and sugar. Add a cup of hot water, cover and simmer over medium heat until all the water evaporates. The sauce should be thick and tasty.

In the meantime, cut the eggplants lengthwise (4-5 thick slices from each). Place the slices in a bowl, sprinkle with salt, cover with water and set aside for 30 minutes. Wash the eggplants under a running tap and dry them with a paper towel. Fry the slices (preferably in olive oil, or any seed oil) until they are golden brown. Place a layer of eggplant in a pyrex container followed by a layer of the sauce and then another layer of eggplant and finally the remaining sauce. Bake in a medium oven, 350°F for 30 minutes.

Note: The judicious use of wholewheat bread to sop up any remains of the sauce is suggested in order to waste as little as possible.

EGGPLANT WITH OLIVE OIL
Melitzanes me Voutyro

Gluten and Dairy-free

1 large eggplant
½ cup olive oil or 4 tablespoonsful polyunsaturated
   margarine
5 cloves of garlic, chopped
1 cup canned tomatoes
½ cup parsley, cnopped
Sea salt and freshly ground black pepper

Cut the eggplant into cubes and put them in a saucepan with cold water and sea salt for 30 minutes to draw out the bitter juices.

In a non-stick saucepan, place the oil or margarine, garlic and eggplant, which should have been thoroughly rinsed and patted with paper towels. Heat and stir constantly for 5 minutes and then add the tomatoes and their juice, the parsley, sea salt, pepper and a cupful of hot water. Simmer until all the water has evaporated and serve warm.

Note: This side dish is ideally served with Skordalia (page 18).

LIMA BEAN STEW
Yigantes Yiahni

(Serves several as a side dish)   *Gluten and Dairy-free*

1 pound lima beans
1½ cups olive oil
2 onions, chopped
½ cup parsley, chopped
2 carrots, chopped
Sea salt and freshly ground black pepper
Pinch of paprika

Soak the beans overnight. Drain and cover with fresh water in a saucepan with a little salt and simmer for 10 minutes. Drain the water and add the olive oil, onion, parsley, carrots, the pepper and a little more salt. Sauté until the onions are soft and golden. Cover with water and allow to cook over low heat until all the liquid has evaporated. Sprinkle with paprika.

ROASTED LIMA BEANS
Yigantes Plaki

This is a traditional, tasty, nourishing dish and carries with it a very Greek flavor.

(Serves 4-6 as a main course or several as a side dish)
Gluten and Dairy-free

1 pound lima beans
½ cup olive oil
½ cup parsley, chopped
1 pound canned tomatoes
6 cloves of garlic, halved lengthwise
2 celery stalks including green leaves, chopped
1½ onions, chopped
2 carrots, chopped
1 teaspoon paprika
Sea salt and freshly ground black pepper

Soak the beans overnight and then, after washing them well, place in boiling water and cook for 30 minutes. At this stage, change the water and continue to cook the beans for another 30 minutes in the new water. (This method effectively destroys enzymes which can produce flatulence and distention.) Place the beans in a pyrex or metal casserole (2-3 inch deep), together with all the other ingredients. Mix well, and cover the mixture with water. Place foil over the container and place in the oven at 425°F for 1 hour. Remove the foil and continue to cook at this heat until all the water has evaporated and the beans are tender, with a degree of browning or crispness to those on the surface. The timing can vary with different qualities of beans and hardness of the water.

BEAN STEW
Fassolakia Yiahni

(Serves 2 as main course, several as a side dish)
Gluten and Dairy-free

1 pound string beans
1½ medium-sized onions, chopped
½ cup olive oil
1 pound canned tomatoes
3 medium-sized potatoes, each cut into 3 or 4 pieces
2 teaspoons chopped parsley
Sea salt and freshly ground black pepper
1 teaspoon raw cane sugar

Trim the beans. Place the chopped onions in a saucepan with the oil and cook until *soft* (*not* until golden or burned). Add the tomatoes and bring to the boil. After 10 minutes add the beans, potatoes, parsley, salt, pepper, sugar and a cup of water. Cover and simmer until all the liquid has evaporated. Serve this dish with wholewheat bread, low-fat cheese and black olives.

Note: Leeks can be used instead of beans in a similar manner except for the use of parsley, which should be omitted; brown rice (which has been pre-boiled) can be used in place of potatoes.

BAKED VEGETABLE STEW
Lahanika Yiahni

(Serves several as a side dish)   *Gluten and Dairy-free*

4 ounces mushrooms
½ pound zucchini
1 eggplant
1 green pepper
2 small potatoes
½ pound string beans
3 large tomatoes, sliced
2 onions, chopped
1 cup parsley, chopped
1 tablespoon raw cane sugar
½ cup olive oil
4 cloves of garlic, chopped
Sea salt and freshly ground black pepper

Wash and chop all the vegetables. Place them in an ovenproof container and add the parsley, sugar, oil, garlic, salt, pepper and a cup of hot water. This should be sufficient liquid as the ingredients add a quantity themselves; however, if the stew is drying out, add a little more water. Bake in a moderate oven at 350°F for 1½ to 2 hours.

Note: Ideally, serve this dish with Skordalia (page 18), lima beans, olives and wholewheat bread.

POTATO CROQUETTES
Kroketes Patates

(Serves several as a side dish)

3 pounds potatoes
4 eggs
¼ cup finely chopped parsley
1 onion, finely chopped
Sea salt and freshly ground black pepper
1 cup grated hard cheese
Wholewheat pastry flour
Vegetable oil for frying (preferably olive oil)

Scrub the potatoes and boil them in their skins in salted water. When soft, peel and mash them while still hot. Make a purée mixture by adding 1 egg and 3 yolks (well beaten), parsley, onion, salt, pepper and cheese and blend thoroughly.

Allow the potatoes to cool and then prepare the croquettes by hand, shaping them into balls. Roll these in the flour before dipping them into the beaten egg white and then again into the flour. When ready, place them on paper towels. Serve hot or cold.

Note: These croquettes can be made without first dipping them into the egg white. When the croquette is ready, simply roll it in a little flour and fry. Powdered rye crispbreads can be used instead of the flour.

SPINACH CROQUETTES
Kroketes Spanaki

(Serves several as a side dish)

2 pounds spinach
1 onion, very finely chopped
1⅓ tablespoons polyunsaturated margarine
1½ cups grated hard cheese
3 eggs
Sea salt and freshly ground black pepper
1¼ cups wholewheat breadcrumbs
1½ cups powdered rye crispbread

Wash the spinach well and steam it until soft. Place in a colander and drain before shredding it into small pieces. Place the shredded spinach in a mixing bowl and add the chopped onion, melted margarine, cheese, 1 egg and 2 egg yolks, sea salt, pepper and the breadcrumbs.

Mix all these ingredients thoroughly. Place the crispbread powder on a plate. Beat the 2 egg whites with 2 teaspoons of water. With the hands, shape 2 heaping tablespoons of the spinach mixture into balls or croquettes and then roll these in the rye powder before dipping in the white of the egg, and again in the rye powder. Fry the croquettes in oil or margarine until all sides look crispy. Serve hot for crispness, or cold for extra flavor.

Note: This may be used as a side dish and can accompany any meal. It can also be used as a mezze, in which case make each croquette much smaller. If whole rye crispbreads are not available, plain wholewheat flour can be used instead.

ZUCCHINI CROQUETTES
Keftedes me Kolokithia

(Serves several as a side dish)

2½ pounds small zucchini
1 cup powdered rye crispbread
1 cup grated hard cheese
3 eggs
1 medium-sized onion, very finely chopped
½ cup parsley, finely chopped
Sea salt and freshly ground black pepper
1⅓ tablespoons polyunsaturated margarine

For frying:
Wholewheat pastry flour
Oil (preferably olive oil)
Sea salt and freshly ground black pepper

Wash and boil the zucchini in salted water. When soft, remove, place in a colander and allow them to drain well. Place them in a mixing bowl and mash with a fork before adding all the other ingredients. Mix well. The result should have a thick consistency; if not, add more crispbread crumbs or wholewheat flour.

Form the mixture into croquettes by hand. Roll these in seasoned flour and fry until golden. Serve hot or cold.

CHICKPEA CROQUETTES
Revithia Kroketes

(Serves several as a side dish)   *Dairy-free*

1¾ cups chickpeas (soaked in water for 1½ days)
1 cup wholewheat pastry flour
1 large onion, finely chopped or grated
1½ cups parsley, finely chopped
1 cup wholewheat bread (soaked and squeezed out)
3 scallions
Sea salt and freshly ground black pepper
Olive oil for frying

Soak the chickpeas in water for 1½ days, remembering to change the water 2-3 times. Rinse well, trying to get rid of the skins of the peas. Place in a saucepan with water and boil for 1 hour. Drain and mash them into a creamy texture. Add 1⅓ tablespoons of the flour and the rest of the ingredients. Mix well and form into balls or croquettes. Dip these in the flour and fry them in pure olive oil until golden.

Note: Serve with Tjatjiki (page 20), lettuce and tomato salad, black olives and wholewheat bread.

9. Cooked Salads

Many vegetables are more nutritious when cooked than in their raw state. This is because cellulose, which binds some of the constituents, is broken down in the cooking process. Overcooking, especially if the fluid is not also ingested, is undersirable because of the loss of essential minerals. Steaming is an ideal method of cooking since it ensures the retention of these minerals and also produces lightly cooked, crisp and delicious vegetables. The use of cooked vegetables, served cold, individually or mixed, is perhaps a novel idea to some. In Greece it is common. The taste of cooked salads can be marvelous and the nutritive value high. My advice is always to slightly undercook rather than the opposite.

POTATO SALAD
Potatosalata

(Serves 4 as a side dish)

4 large potatoes
1 onion, sliced
16 black olives
Sea salt
½ cup olive oil
⅓ cup wine or cider vinegar
1 teaspoon oregano
Fresh parsley

Boil the potatoes in their skins. When cooked, peel them and place in a shallow dish. Allow them to cool and then cut into slices. Put sliced onions between the slices of potatoes. Add the olives and dress with salt, oil, vinegar and oregano. Garnish with the parsley and serve warm or cold as a side dish.

BEET SALAD
Batzaria Salata

(Serves 4 as a side dish)

2 large or 4 small beets
1 large onion, sliced or 4 cloves of garlic thinly sliced
½ cup olive oil
½ cup wine or cider vinegar
Sea salt
Fresh parsley

Peel and slice the cooked beets and place the overlapping slices around the sides of a shallow container. To each slice add either a slice of onion or a slice of garlic (not both). Dress with oil and vinegar and a little salt, and garnish with parsley. Serve warm or cold.

Note: Beets contain significant amounts of calcium, iron and phosphorus as well as vitamins A, C and some of the vital B vitamins. Their health-promoting qualities are many and they should be a major part of salad meals, grated raw or cooked, as above.

CAULIFLOWER SALAD
Kounoupidi

As a member of the cabbage family, cauliflower is rich in sulphur, calcium, iron and phosphorus. Known in healing circles as a blood purifier, it encourages detoxification. It is a useful vegetable, raw or cooked. The quantity of cauliflower depends on the number of people to be served. When buying a cauliflower, choose one which is firm and white. Its firmness will ensure crispness and its whiteness will ensure freshness.

For a dressing:

Olive oil
Lemon juice
Black pepper (touch)
Sea salt

Cut the cauliflower into quarters, wash well and place in a steamer. Steam for no longer than 8 minutes, to ensure that the crispness is not lost and the nutritive value is retained as far as possible.

Dressing:
Mix 2 parts oil to 1 part lemon, with a little pepper and sea salt, pour onto the cauliflower and serve hot or cold.

MIXED VEGETABLE SALAD
Lahanika Anamikta

Gluten and Dairy-free
This type of cooked salad provides a rich supply of essential minerals, vegetable fiber and vitamins. It should play a regular part in the balanced wholefood diet.

1 carrot, well washed and sliced
4 ounces string beans, trimmed
½ fennel, washed and cut into large pieces
1 globe artichoke (see instructions on preparation of artichokes, page 60) cut into 8 pieces
4 ounces peas
1 potato, cut into 6 pieces
1 celery stalk, sliced and with strings removed
1 small beet, undercooked and diced
10 black olives
1 small Spanish onion

For the dressing:
Olive oil
Wine or cider vinegar
Oregano
Sea salt

Place the first six vegetables in the steamer. Steam for 10 minutes and then add the celery and steam for another 5 minutes. Empty all the ingredients into a serving dish. Add the diced beet, the olives and the raw onion. Add the dressing with 2 parts oil, 1 part vinegar, the oregano and salt. Mix well, but gently.

DANDELIONS AND FENNEL
Prikalida ke Marathro

Dandelions grow almost everywhere. In some countries the dandelion is considered a weed. In Greece, it is cultivated and sold in the markets. This delicious and most edible plant contains many minerals and it has a deserved reputation as a cleanser of the liver. Seeds are available in the market and a corner of any garden could be put aside for their cultivation.

Pick the desired quantity and wash them well. Put water and a little sea salt in a saucepan and bring to the boil. Add the dandelions and fennel (which should have been cut into 8 pieces). Cook the vegetables until tender (approx. 15 minutes). Serve hot or cold and dress with lemon juice and olive oil. Finely chopped garlic also complements this dish.

DANDELION JUICE

The water in which the dandelions have been cooked is very good to drink. It contains the essence and has a high mineral content. This is an excellent natural diuretic and liver stimulant. In a cup containing the dandelion water add the juice of half a lemon and a tablespoon of olive oil. Drink hot or cold, at any time of the day, or before going to bed. The juice of zucchini, zucchini tops and turnip tops, can be used in the same way.

The content of dandelion leaves includes a very high vitamin A and C concentration and some of the B vitamins, as well as high iron, potassium and calcium levels. It has been used widely in treating rheumatic conditions, anemia, digestive complaints, diabetes and kidney ailments.

TURNIP TOPS
Goggilia

This plant, which grows easily in any garden, is highly nutritious. It contains a very high concentration of potassium and calcium as well as vitamins A, C, E and K in good quantities. This vegetable is very suitable for young and old as a health-enhancing part of a wholefood diet.

Pick as many tops as are required. Steam and dress with a mixture of olive oil, lemon juice and sea salt. Serve warm or cold as a side dish.

ZUCCHINI TOPS
Kolokithokorfades

Greeks, especially those who don't live in big cities, look forward to the end of the zucchini season when they will find, in the market, zucchini tops! These are very rich in minerals and enzymes and aid liver function. It would, of course, be ideal to grow one's own zucchini as this ensures that there has been no spraying.

Zucchini tops are the young tender leaves of the zucchini plant, its very heart. These are only picked when the plant stops producing any more zucchini. Pick the desired quantity, wash well, and steam to the desired tenderness (only a few minutes). Serve warm or cold and dress with olive oil, a little sea salt and lemon juice or wine vinegar.

Note: This vegetable is traditionally served with Skordalia (page 18).

BEET TOPS
Batzaria

Not many non-Greeks know that beet tops are not only edible and very tasty but extremely nourishing. They can either be picked from the garden when young and tender, or bought with uncooked roots. Any yellow leaves should be discarded. Wash well and add the beet tops to a saucepan of boiling salted water an inch deep. Cook until tender (but do not overcook – approximately 10 minutes).

For a dressing:
Olive oil and vinegar are ideal. Serve with Skordalia (page 18).

COOKED GREEN SALADS
Prasines Vrastes Salates

Fresh beans or zucchini or endive or spinach and carrots may be used in a cooked salad. The vegetables should be cooked as follows in order to ensure little loss of food value and retention of flavor.

Place the vegetables in a steamer and cook until they begin to become tender (test with a fork from time to time). Serve with a dressing made of lemon juice or wine vinegar, olive oil (2 parts oil to 1 part vinegar or lemon), and sea salt. Any other oil could be used, if preferred. Oregano may be added to the dressing when zucchini and carrots are used. Crushed garlic may be added for any vegetable of the cabbage family and zucchini. Decorate with black olives. Serve as a side dish, hot or cold.

LIMA BEAN SALAD
Yigantes Salata

(Serves several as a side dish)   *Gluten and Dairy-free*

¾ pound lima beans
2 tablespoons minced parsley
6 scallions, chopped
10 black olives
¾ cup olive oil
¼ cup lemon juice
Sea salt and freshly ground black pepper
Watercress, chopped

Soak the beans overnight. Wash them well and boil for 15 minutes. Change the water and allow them to cook until tender. Five minutes before removing from the heat, add a little sea salt. Drain, allow to cool, place in a bowl and add all the ingredients except the watercress. Cover and when completely cool mix gently. Add the watercress before serving.

Note: Oregano may be used instead of parsley and wine vinegar instead of lemon juice, if preferred.

STUFFED ARTICHOKES
Agginares Gemistes me Hortarika

Gluten and Dairy-free
This dish can be served as a starter or side dish. It is an ideal accompaniment for any other vegetables and for any of the recipes in this book.

Artichokes
Carrots
Peas

For the dressing:
Mix thoroughly ¾ cup of olive oil, ¼ cup of lemon juice, sea salt, black pepper, very finely chopped parsley and very finely chopped scallion.

Choose very tender artichokes. Cut off the stalk and remove the choke using a sharp knife. The outer leaves are left intact as, in a young artichoke, these will be edible. Boil the artichokes with the carrots and peas in salted water until tender. Remove from the heat and allow to cool.

Mix the dressing. Stuff the artichokes with 4-5 slices of carrot and 2 teaspoons of peas and then pour on 2-3 tablespoons of the dressing. Serve warm or cold.

ZUCCHINI FLOWERS
Kolokytholoulouda

The flowers of the zucchini or summer squash plant are a delicacy. They can be eaten raw in a salad or, if stuffing them (page 79) is too much trouble, then they can be steamed. After washing carefully (they are very delicate), steam them for no more than 1½ minutes. When cooked, dress with olive oil, lemon juice and sea salt and serve, ideally with Skordalia (page 18).

10. Cakes and Desserts

STRAWBERRIES WITH ORANGE JUICE AND BRANDY
Fraoles me Himo Portokali ke Koniac

Quantities should be adapted as required, but for, let us say, 1 pound of strawberries, this dessert should be prepared as follows:

1 pound strawberries
¼ cup brandy
½ cup fresh orange juice
⅓ raw cane sugar (optional)

Wash the strawberries in cold water. Mix the brandy and orange juice together. Place a layer of strawberries in a bowl, then sprinkle with a little raw cane sugar and pour a few drops of the juice-brandy mixture over the top. Carefully, so as not to bruise the fruit, lift and mix the ingredients. Continue in the same way, adding the fruit, sugar and juice until they are all used up and well mixed. Refrigerate for 2 hours before serving. Serve in open champagne glasses or glass bowls.

NEW YEAR'S DAY CAKE
Vassilopita

1 cupful polyunsaturated margarine
1 cup dark brown sugar
5 eggs
3 teaspoons baking powder
½ wine glass Grand Marnier or plain brandy
Rinds of 2 oranges and 2 lemons
¾ cup peeled and ground almonds
¾ cup currants and raisins, mixed
½ cup milk
Juice of ½ orange
Sesame seeds
2½ cups wholewheat pastry flour

Place the margarine and the sugar in a mixing bowl. Mix well to a smooth consistency. Add the yolks of the eggs. When well blended, add the baking powder, diluted in the brandy first, finely grated lemon and orange rinds, ground almonds, the raisins and the milk. The contents should be mixed constantly.

In the meantime, beat the whites of the eggs to form frothy peaks. Add to the basic mixture a little of the egg and orange juice until all the ingredients are used. Place in a buttered cake pan, sprinkle with sesame seeds and bake in a hot oven at 425°F for 50 minutes. Allow to cool before removing from the pan.

Note: More and/or different nuts may be used, such as walnuts. The number of the new year is usually written on the surface of the cake with sesame seeds or split almonds, prior to cooking. Traditionally, a golden coin (sovereign) was hidden in the Vassilopita, and, of course, the lucky finder kept this as a souvenir.

YOGURT CAKE
Keik me Yiaourti

1½ cups raw cane sugar
1 cup butter or polyunsaturated margarine
6 ounces plain goat's yogurt
5 eggs
3 cups wholewheat pastry flour
2 teaspoons baking powder
3 tablespoons grated lemon and/or orange rind

In a mixing bowl, place the sugar and butter and blend until smooth. Add the yogurt and mix well. Beat the egg yolks and add them to the mixture. In the meantime, beat the egg whites well. Add to the mixture a little of the flour, baking powder, a little of the lemon rind and a little of the egg white. Continue mixing and repeat until all the ingredients are used.

Empty the mixture into a large oiled loaf pan and place in a medium to hot oven at 375°F for approximately 1 hour. Allow to cool before removing from the tin.

Note: To check if the cake is done (this applies to any cake) stick a knife into it. If the knife comes out dry, the cake is ready. If it comes out with small crumbs of cake on it, it needs further cooking.

Variation: Peeled and grated almonds and/or walnuts (½-⅓ cup) may be added to the basic cake mixture, if liked.

EXOTIC FRUIT SALAD
Exotiki Froutosalata

The following fruit salad is a memorable end to a meal.
Use any of the following fruits that are available.

Guavas
Chinese gooseberries
Pineapple
Lychees
Bananas
Passion Fruit
Papaya
Mangos
Juice of tangerines or grapes

According to the required quantity, chop up the above
fruits into a serving bowl. Empty the pulp of the passion
fruit, and pour on the juice of the tangerines or grapes.
Mix gently and refrigerate for 1-2 hours. Serve on its own.

FRUIT SALAD
Froutosalata

This salad can be made at any time of the year and it is
delicious and nourishing. Quantities should be according
to requirements.

Wash the fruit well. Peel peaches, bananas, pears and
apples, remove the seeds from melon, grapes and cherries
and cut everything into small pieces. Place in serving
bowl and add a little raw cane sugar, if desired. Squeeze
the juice of a lemon over the fruit (this is to slow down the
oxidation process which discolors fruit). Mix well but
gently. Add a small quantity of brandy to the salad with
some fresh walnuts. Mix, cover, and refrigerate for 2-3
hours before serving. Serve with natural yogurt or soy
milk as a dressing, if liked.

11. Children's Recipes

A combination of legumes and cereals offers a balance that contains all the essential amino acids (the building blocks of protein); for example, lentils and brown rice, or beans and millet. To provide a variety of minerals and vitamins and to obtain variations in flavor, vegetables in season are widely used in these recipes. The resultant mixture contains complete vegetable protein, vitamins A, B_1, B_3 (niacin), folic acid, potassium, calcium, phosphorus, iron, etc., as well as the necessary vegetable fiber which guarantees healthy bowel function.

The nutritional values of some of the ingredients mentioned in these recipes are as follows:

Millet
9 per cent protein, 4 per cent fat, 70 per cent carbohydrate.
Rich in: potassium, magnesium, iron, phosphorus.

Lentils
25.7 per cent protein, 1.9 per cent fat, 53 per cent carbohydrate.
Rich in: potassium, sodium, calcium, iron, phosphorus.

Chickpeas
13 per cent protein, 1.6 per cent fat, 50 per cent carbohydrate.
Rich in: potassium, magnesium, calcium, phosphorus.

Brown Rice
8 per cent protein, 8 per cent fat, 70 per cent carbohydrate.
Rich in: potassium, magnesium, phosphorus.

Lima beans
7 per cent protein, 1 per cent fat, 18 per cent carbohydrate.
Rich in: minerals and B vitamins.

The recipes below are suitable for any child from nine
months or so onwards. Depending upon the child's
ability to chew, the thickness of the mixtures should be
varied. For a young baby, a food processor provides the
ideal texture of food. The cereal and legume dishes as
described below can, for an older child, be prepared as a
loaf. The lentil and rice or lentil and millet dish with the
addition of some milled nuts and wholewheat breadcrumbs
can be placed in a tin and baked into a loaf. Where seeds
and nuts are required, they should always be prepared in a
processor.

Some ideas for a day's menu for a child of 18 months to 3 years:

Breakfast: Fresh juice of 1-2 oranges
Nut, Seed, Fruit, Yogurt and Honey Delight
(page 121)
Alternate days, 1 boiled egg
Glass of milk (soy)

Lunch: Spinach, Rice and Chick-Pea dish (page 120)
Grated raw carrot
Grated raw beet
1 piece of fresh fruit
Glass of pure fruit juice, soy milk, or water

Evening: Egg and Potato dish (page 122), with salad
or steamed vegetables or Nut, Seed, Fruit,
Yogurt and Honey Delight (page 121)

Before sleep: Glass of warm soy milk with molasses or a
little honey

RICE, LENTILS AND VEGETABLES
Ryzi-Fakes ke Horta

(Serves 3)   *Gluten and Dairy-free*

½ cup lentils
½ cup brown rice
2 carrots
1 tomato
1 celery stalk   } chopped
2 mushrooms
1 clove of garlic, crushed
2 teaspoons olive oil
1 cube clear vegetable bouillon (optional)

Soak the lentils overnight, rinse well and place in a saucepan with 2 cups of water. Cook over medium heat until the lentils soften and then add all other ingredients and cover with water. Simmer until all the water has evaporated. Place the contents in a blender and reduce to a creamy texture. Brown rice may, depending upon its type or on the quality of water, require extra cooking and it is advisable to cook it on its own for approximately 20 minutes before adding it to the mixture.

LENTILS, MILLET AND VEGETABLES
Fakes – Kehri ke Lahanika

(Serves 3-4)   *Dairy-free*

½ cup lentils
½ cup millet
2 carrots
1 zucchini
½ onion   } chopped
1 tomato
1 small potato, scrubbed and chopped (most of its
   value lies just under the skin)
2 tablespoons olive oil
⅓ teaspoon oregano
Sea salt

Prepare the lentils as in the recipe for Rice, Lentils and
Vegetables (page 117), then add all the other ingredients
and simmer until the water has evaporated. Blend to a
consistency suitable for the child (i.e. creamy before
teeth are present and more "lumpy" when chewing is
possible).

CHICKPEAS, MILLET AND VEGETABLES
Revithia – Kehri ke Lahanika

(Serves 3-4 – according to the age of the child)
Dairy-free

¾ cup chickpeas
½ cup millet
2 tablespoons olive oil
⅓ teaspoon rosemary
1 tomato } chopped
2 carrots }
1 zucchini or 2 fresh asparagus or 1 artichoke
Sea salt

I find that chickpeas require much more soaking and cooking than lentils. Soak these overnight and cook over medium heat until tender, then add the other ingredients and follow the same procedure as for previous recipes.

LIMA BEANS AND MILLET WITH VEGETABLES
Fassolia Yigantes me Lahanika

(Serves 3) *Dairy-free*

¾ cup lima beans
½ cup millet
2 leeks
1 medium or large tomato
1 onion } chopped
2 carrots }
1 celery stalk
1⅓ tablespoons olive oil
Sea salt

Soak the beans overnight. Simmer for 45 minutes. Add all the other ingredients and cover with water. Simmer until all the water has evaporated. Reduce to a creamy texture for very young children.

SPINACH, RICE, CHICKPEAS AND VEGETABLES
Spanaki – Ryzi – Revithia – Hortarika

(Serves up to 4 meals, according to the age of the child)
Gluten and Dairy-free

1 pound spinach
½ cup brown rice
¾ cup chickpeas
2 carrots
1 clove of garlic and/or 3 scallions
3 tablespoons parsley
1⅔ tablespoons olive oil
1 artichoke (optional)
Sea salt

Soak the chickpeas overnight. Change the water and simmer until tender. Add the rice and simmer 15 minutes before adding all the other ingredients. Cover with water and prepare as for previous recipes.

NUT, SEED, FRUIT, YOGURT AND HONEY DELIGHT
Karydia me Frouta ke Yiaourti

Gluten-free
The following makes one large helping. A six-month-old child would be satisfied with half this quantity as a main course.

1 walnut
4 almonds
1 teaspoon sunflower seeds
and/or pumpkin seeds

For an infant these must be reduced to powder in a food processor. For an older child they can be grated finely

½ a peach or nectarine or pear or apple
4 grapes
¼ avocado
½ to 1 banana
2 teaspoons pure honey
3-4 ounces goat's milk yogurt

The seeds and nuts are prepared first in a processor and then the fruit is added to reduce the contents to a creamy purée. Place in a bowl, add the yogurt and honey and mix well with a spoon.

This is a nutritious and delicious mixture containing all the value of complete protein as well as vitamin C, B, and minerals such as iron and calcium. It is a complete meal for a baby and a dessert for an older child.

EGGS WITH POTATOES
Avga me Patatas Poure

(Serves 2-3)   *Gluten-free*

2 pounds potatoes
1 cup cow's or goat's or soy milk
1½ cups grated hard cheese
6 eggs
2⅔ tablespoons polyunsaturated margarine
Sea salt and freshly ground black pepper

Cook the potatoes and mash them with the milk and margarine. Oil the sides of a 10 inch baking dish and sprinkle some of the grated cheese on the bottom. Add the mashed potato and make six holes, into which the eggs should be broken whole. Season and sprinkle the remaining grated cheese on top and after putting a little melted margarine over each egg, bake in a hot oven at 425°F for 10 minutes.

Note: This dish could be complemented with grated raw beet, grated carrot, a sliced tomato and watercress or steamed vegetables such as carrots, peas, cauliflower, mushrooms, etc., dressed with a little sea salt, olive oil and lemon juice.

12. Balancing the Diet

Among the many Greek sayings is one that translates: "A healthy mind in a healthy body". A healthy and strong body can be built with the help of a balanced diet, and variety is important, not just for the sake of providing interesting meals.

My suggestion is that once you have become accustomed to the recipes in this book (especially those that will freeze well), then make them again in larger quantities and keep them in the freezer. This will enable you to stock up on a number of meals, which will conveniently bring a variety of wholefood goodness to the table.

While initially the preparation of the variety of foods suggested in the week's menu that follows will entail a great deal of cooking, the use of the freezer to store the surplus will mean many weeks of reduced labor. I find it so, and with a little thought and planning the freezer can be kept well stocked.

The general pattern of eating should be such that 50 per cent or more of the diet comprises raw foods such as salad, fruit, seeds, nuts and cereals. Breakfast should be a fruit, seed, nut and cereal meal. One of the main meals should be a salad-based meal with wholewheat bread or potato salad. The other main meal should contain protein and vegetables. Desserts should consist of fresh or dried fruit. Fruit and seeds (e.g. sunflower) make handy snacks.

Drinks should be taken between meals and consist of either fresh fruit juice or spring water.

Sunday

Lunch
Mixed Salad
Tjatjiki (Yogurt and
Cucumber Dip)
Chick-Pea Croquettes
Fried Artichokes
Choice of fruit

Dinner
Artichoke Moussaka
Mixed Grilled Vegetables
Skordalia (Garlic Potato)
Choice of fruit

Monday

Lunch
Peasant Salad
Potato Salad
Féta or cottage cheese
Wholewheat bread
Choice of fruit

Dinner
Macaroni Pie
Roasted Lima Beans
Choice of steamed vegetables
Choice of fruit

Tuesday

Lunch
Salad Lettuce with Eggs
Tjatjiki (Yogurt and
Cucumber Dip)
Sliced tomatoes
Wholewheat bread
Cottage cheese
Choice of fruit

Dinner
Millet Pie
Skordalia (Garlic Potato)
Beet Salad
Choice of steamed vegetables
Choice of fruit

Wednesday

Lunch
Cucumber Salad
Hummus
Wholewheat bread
Rice with Golden Raisins
Nuts
Fruit

Dinner
Artichokes Vinaigrette
Wholewheat bread
Choice of cheeses
Choice of fruit
Yogurt and honey

Thursday

Lunch
Mixed Salad
Lima Bean Salad
Rice with Golden Raisins
Wholewheat bread
Choice of fruit

Dinner
Moussaka with Eggplant
Skordalia (Garlic Potato)
Chickpea Croquettes
Choice of steamed vegetables
Choice of fruit

Friday

Lunch
Fresh salad
Eggplant Dip
Wholewheat bread
Potato Salad

Dinner
Lentil Soup
Wholewheat toast
Choice of cheeses
Choice of fruit

Saturday

Lunch
Fresh mixed salad
Potato Croquettes
Tjatjiki (Yogurt and
Cucumber Dip)
Wholewheat bread
Choice of fruit

Dinner
Stuffed Tomatoes with Eggs
Brown rice
Lima beans
Skordalia (Garlic Potato)
Steamed vegetables
Choice of fruit

Breakfast throughout the week may comprise of one of the following cominations:

1. Overnight soak the following in water: 2 to 4 teaspoons each of oat flakes, sesame seeds, linseed, pumpkin seeds and 2 or 3 ounces dried fruit (cut into pieces). In the morning, add 2 to 4 teaspoons of sunflower seeds, wheat germ, unprocessed bran (optional) and walnuts or almonds. Add a grated apple or a sliced banana or some grapes. Natural (live) yogurt may also be eaten with this dish.

2. Fresh walnuts and/or almonds and honey, yogurt and fresh fruit, with wholewheat breat or toast and a yeast spread (such as Marmite, etc.); a sugarless jam can be added, if still hungry.

Index